Additional Praise for *Sanity and Grace*

"Judy Collins shares her pain and her faith with us so courageously that we are all left stronger and more hopeful for reading it."

—RABBI HAROLD KUSHNER, author of
When Bad Things Happen to Good People

"*Sanity and Grace* is a breath-stopping tale of pain; a superb treatise on the indelible, blighting aftereffects of suicide, and yet a profoundly affirming hymn to life—the mundane, daily life of the body and the tremulous, hope-filled, at times exalted life of the spirit. Judy Collins has given us an achingly honest, powerful book."

—MAGGIE SCARF, author of *Intimate Partners*

"Judy's story is a journey of the spirit and a powerful teacher proving that from adversity comes great opportunity . . . not just to survive what life sends our way, but to thrive in the sanity and grace that come from staying the course of recovery."

—WILLIAM C. MOYERS, Head of Public Information,
Hazelden Foundation

"Brutally honest, eloquently written. Judy Collins shares her poignant journey of surviving her beloved son's suicide. She shows her passion for life, her struggle and courage to keep singing through and beyond the pain . . . to keep living. Her curiosity and indomitable spirit enhance the readers ability to achieve hope and to survive their own traumas. . . with sanity and grace."

—IRIS BOLTON, author of *My Son . . . My Son . . . A Guide
to Healing After Death, Loss, or Suicide*

"Judy Collins was dealt one of life's worst blows in the suicide of her beloved son, Clark. She has dealt with that tragedy heroically in her beautifully written book, *Sanity and Grace*. I was both moved to tears and filled with the most enormous admiration for her as she depicted the phases of grief that ultimately led to her ability to go on with her life. There is beauty in this book"

—DOMINICK DUNNE

"In her intelligent and painful study, Judy examines every aspect of suicide. She does so comprehensively, from the vantage of one whose only son killed himself . . . and of one who herself is filled with tendencies. The references beyond herself are exhaustively researched and will sound a chord in every reader, because every reader has—to some extent—heard the self-destructive call. In *Sanity and Grace* Judy Collins has written an achingly human book. It is painful, sweet, and redemptive. Out of her own devastation, she has created beauty and solace. She gives comfort, hope. She gives herself. Which is a gift both rich and of extraordinary tenderness."

—JERROLD MUNDIS, author of *Gerhardt's Children and the Dogs*

"Judy's book showed me what I did not know I knew. It did not change me so much as reveal me to myself."

—NED ROREM

"Judy Collins has written a delicate and powerful book on a delicate and powerful subject. Her words pour the balm of compassion on victim and survivor alike."

—JULIA CAMERON, author of *The Artist's Way*

"Once again, Judy provides us with light, love, and directions for a dark subject that requires her unique voice."

—JEANNETTE MASON, psychotherapist, author, survivor, and founder of Survivors of Loved Ones' Suicide

Sanity *and* Grace

ALSO BY JUDY COLLINS:

Trust Your Heart

Singing Lessons

Shameless

Voices

Amazing Grace

The Judy Collins Songbook

JEREMY P. TARCHER • PENGUIN

A MEMBER OF

PENGUIN GROUP (USA) INC.

NEW YORK

Sanity *and* Grace

A Journey of SUICIDE,
SURVIVAL, *and*
STRENGTH

JUDY COLLINS

Certain names and identifying characteristics have been changed to protect
the privacy of the individuals involved.

Most Tarcher/Penguin books are available at special quantity discounts for
bulk purchase for sales promotions, premiums, fund-raising, and educational needs. Special books or book excerpts also can be created to fit spe-
cific needs. For details, write Penguin Group (USA) Inc. Special Markets,
375 Hudson Street, New York, NY 10014.

Jeremy P. Tarcher/Penguin
a member of
Penguin Group (USA) Inc.
375 Hudson Street
New York, NY 10014
www.penguin.com

Library of Congress Cataloging-in-Publication Data

Collins, Judy, date.
Sanity and grace : a journey of suicide, survival, and strength / Judy Collins.
p.   cm.
Includes bibliographical references.
ISBN 1-58542-261-4
I. Collins, Judy, date.   2. Singers—United States—Biography.   I. Title
ML420.C65A3   2003   2003050755
782.42164'092—dc21

Printed in the United States of America
1   3   5   7   9   10   8   6   4   2

This book is printed on acid-free paper. ∞

Book design by Deborah Kerner / Dancing Bears Design

To Chuck, my father,

whose inner vision was perfect.

To Clark, my son,

who saw so much.

To Hollis, my granddaughter,

the apple of my eye,

who will see the world in a new way.

Acknowledgments

My thanks to Al Lowman, my agent, who has believed in this book and helped me believe in it; BG Dillworth at Authors and Artists; Joel Fotinos, my publisher at Tarcher, who gave me such strong and consistent support; Allison Sobel, my editor; Victoria Pearson, copyeditor; George Furth, who supported me with his insight and humor in every way, and also led me to Professor Edwin Shneidman; Katherine De Paul, my gifted assistant and Major Domo; Bridget Maybury and everyone at Rocky Mountain Productions and Wildflower Records; Kelly Groves, my publicist at Tarcher; Shoena Valeska, photographer; Jerry Mundis, my writing coach, who insisted I keep writing when I wanted to put this book away and never see it again; Julia Cameron, who believed in this book. I am grateful to my beloved family, near and far—my mother, Marjorie; sister, Holly; brothers Denver, David, and Michael; stepfather Robert; my brother-in-law, sisters-in-law, nephews, nieces, and extended family; Hollis, Clark's daughter and my granddaughter, and Hollis's maternal family—her mother Alyson, grandmother

Sandy, and aunt Robin; Peter Taylor, Clark's father; Hadley Taylor Fisk, my former sister-in-law and friend; Gary Taylor, Clarke's uncle; Maryanne Goodman and the memory of Clark's cousin, Luke; and all Clark's paternal family.

I also wish to extend thanks to Iris Bolton, Joan Rivers, Gloria Vanderbilt, Patricia Bosworth, Mariette Hartley, A. Alvarez, Geo Stone, and Sue Chance, who had the courage to write about their experiences with suicide, and all who have lived through both the secrets and the survival of suicide with open hearts and great courage. Warmest appreciation to my friends, especially Susan Cheever, Jeanette Mason, Loretta Barrett, Nancy Bacal, Virginia Dwan, Jane Cecil, Virginia Mailman, and Erica Jong, who have read the book in its many stages, and given me the confidence to finish. Thanks, as well, to Muriel Lloyd for lending back my watercolor for the book jacket!

And to my best friend and husband, Louis Nelson. I love you.

Thank you all. I could not have done this without you.

Contents

Preface

I have written *Sanity and Grace* to shed more light upon the dark taboo of suicide. The suicide of my son was devastating beyond words, yet here I am again, trying to put everything I know or have read or heard or thought about suicide into words, for my own healing as well as that of others.

In writing and thinking about the subject, it has become clear to me that even with the popularity of books and movies about suicide, such as *The Hours* and *Savage God*, and the dedicated work of survivors and professionals alike, the taboo is strong and growing. It is my hope that *Sanity and Grace* may bring hope to those who are in need of solutions for suicide—that is, finally, to all of us.

When my son died, I made the decision that I would live every day as if it were my last—every moment to the hilt. As the years since my son's death have passed, and I have continued to grow and create, the question often arises from friends or acquaintances, "What are you working on at the moment?" Among the records and new songs, the television specials and other gifts that life has offered, seemingly more after my son's awful passing, I answer that I am also working on the subject of suicide—my own experiences, as well as others'—a sort of monograph of tears but also of research on loss, and lessons from other survivors. A gasp often greets this information, then a tone of recognition and perhaps fear. Then, if the talk continues, people remember "their" suicide—the one in the family no one ever mentioned but everyone sensed, the dark, forbidden territory of the psyche, the mother, child, the father, cousin, the sister, the friend. What follows is usually deep and curious, like walking on the moon, and then strangely familiar, like walking in your own living room. I have found that people want and need to explore this subject in their own lives, that the discussion brings needed relief—to all of us. For we all, being human, have some suicide story in our past or our future.

One day, suicide might attain the normality, in a sense, of heart disease or lung ailments, diabetes or cancer. We might be able to say, "Here is the situation medically and psychiatrically, now what can be done to prevent it? To cure it?" And if, as with some diseases, the cure is impossible, then the dignity of respect, the honor of understanding, may be bestowed upon the suicide and his or her family. Otherwise no sacred act is really sacred, when we condemn a sick and suffering soul to secrecy and render them lost, and ourselves sick, from the secret of their passing.

This book is for all of those who are gone, and for all of us as well, those who remember and those who try to forget.

The sacred is always expressed in remembrance.

There was a pause — just long enough for an angel to pass, flying slowly.

It was as though time stopped, the clocks stopped and I stepped into the gap, walking into it as though it were a mansion with many rooms. It was all right that you were gone, because it was only a minor detail and some bright and sweet and soft angel was saying those details are not important, there is here there, there here; it is all one and the same.

And I planned the rest of my life, and then stopped planning, because I knew it was not the point, that love was the point, that all was love, and you were love and I am and we are and no passing terrible thing can alter that, that only a perception of something between the gaps can sustain us, nourish us. The moment of stopped time is the most important of all, it is what counts, not the other.

I will live in the gap, live in the moment between the breaths, in that pause where wings of an angel pass, where the flowers bloom, where love is born out of trouble.

Let me stay in the moment, in that place of timeless wonder.

CHAPTER I

Whales *and* Nightingales

The Heron

In the vapors of the lake
At dusk
One single Heron
Stood, a whiteness on the shore.
Alone, his wings spread
And in flight he filled my vision
So that it was only him I saw.
The lake, it was, that
Flew away.

—JUDY COLLINS

The first time I remember hearing the word "suicide" was a lazy spring afternoon in Denver, Colorado, in 1949. I had come home from school. My father was there in his big easy chair, running his fingers over the pages of a Braille book, a glass of whiskey at his elbow, the ice slowly melting. My father's drinks never got too watered.

This particular day was one of those quiet afternoons when I was reading and my father was stirring the ice cubes in his drink with his index finger, making that clinking sound that could mean a mellow night, or a horror show. We never knew. The prelude was usually calm, full of intelligent conversation and good stories, reading, listening to music. But Daddy fought his own demons, mostly in front of me and my mother, Marjorie, and my siblings.

It was that afternoon that he told me about the suicide. We were sitting in the living room of our red brick duplex on Willow Street. I listened eagerly to Daddy's voice, probably glad to put off my inevitable daily date with the keyboard. I was ten.

Daddy was reading from a big Braille copy of *Moby-Dick*. With his fingers, he caressed the thick pages as though they were made of some fine silk, the raised dots spilling out Melville's epic tale of the greens, rights, sperms, and humpbacked whales, and the journey of Ishmael and Ahab. His smooth baritone voice rose and fell among the gentle noises of the household about us—my mother in the kitchen preparing the evening meal, my three siblings, Mike, David, and Denver the baby intent on the chores and solaces of the afternoon. The fading light splintered and fluttered in the room as the story of *Moby-Dick* unfolded. My mind roamed a thousand miles away, my imagination fired with water and spears, waves and heathen tattoos, ambergris and whaleboats rolling in foam.

My father paused, the story halting in midair like ocean spume, diamonds of water catching the light. His hands fell quiet on the pages of his book. I was left amid the waters of the North Atlantic, a whale ship rigged to chase a pod of females, the spears and tackle ready to fly into bright air. The spell was broken, and as I stirred, taking a sip of my Kool-Aid, green and sweet around my lips, my father's voice rearranged the silence. He cleared his throat and began speaking, this time not reading from the book that lay open on his lap. His voice filled the room as he began another story, that of a man named Al Taylor, a stranger to us, someone whose widow and children we had recently met on moving to Denver from Los Angeles. Al Taylor, it seemed, had taken his own life. He had committed suicide, my father said.

It was the first time I had heard that word spoken. I don't remember having read it, but I somehow knew it was a terrible word, anyway. It was like a small knife in my stomach, and it seemed to sit there, waiting for me to either take it out or call for my mother to take it out. I asked my father who Al Taylor was and why he had committed suicide. For a ten-year-old, I was very smart about suicide, for someone who knew nothing of it.

Daddy told me about Al Taylor. He said Al, whose widow, Margaret, I had met, as well as her children, Peter, Gary, and Hadley, was a successful, seemingly happy man. He wasn't sure why a person like that should take his own life, but there must have been reasons. Maybe he was unhappy, I offered. "Maybe," my father replied. "Maybe."

Many years later, I learned something about Al Taylor, but never much, although his son was, by then, my husband, and my son was his grandson.

Would have been, that is, if Al Taylor were to have lived.

I don't know why my father chose that moment to share the story with me. Perhaps it was the drama of Ahab's obsession, the images of frothing water, men on the hunt for wild giant beasts; perhaps it was the intimacy of the moment we shared in the quiet afternoon. He didn't spare me the details of Al's suicide. Daddy always thought I was man enough to understand that life was not for everyone. He would, in the future, tell me many of his secret stories, about himself, about his longings, his dreams, often during our reading sessions. In school in Boise and Gooding, Idaho, he learned to read and write Braille, type his own scripts for his radio shows, both Braille and script. He played the piano beautifully, and his life had been about survival, about overcoming his handicap, his drinking, his setbacks, and whatever fate threw at him. He had fought his way up and out from under the dirt-farm Idaho childhood, with hard labor and little reward for a life of grueling work, to a life of a good degree of fame, in Seattle, in Los Angeles, and now in Denver. He was a well-known man about town, well read, intent on education and the love of his wife and his five children (my sister Holly was still a spark of light in my parents' imaginations). My father was difficult in many ways, but he was also a successful father, breadwinner, and even, lover. He was committed to life, in all its contrasts, in all its glory, in all its vagaries and mystery.

Daddy would have probably been home most of the afternoon by then, and he might have gotten a little buzz on if he was off the wagon. He would have done his radio show, *Chuck Collins Calling*, which was on the air regularly every weekday in Denver, or on stations in Los Angeles and Seattle, where my family had lived before we moved to Denver in 1949. "On the

Sunny Side of the Street" was the song he used for his theme song, "Grab your coat and get your hat, leave your worries on the doorstep, just direct your feet to the sunny side of the street." He had a sweet and lilting baritone, and so it was usually with the sound of Daddy's voice and his cheer that I would bound out the door, defying the mood of the night before—my parents' fighting, perhaps, or the disputes over money, and over his drinking—with my brownbag lunch of whole-wheat sandwiches. My father gave us lectures on the evils of white rice and white bread, and the glories of Gaylord Hauser's fruit juice and health-food diets, which Daddy used in his efforts to come off his horrific hangovers. So I had whole-wheat bread and peanut butter and chopped carrots or celery and one of my mother Marjorie's big chocolate brownies, for good measure. I think my mother wasn't too sure about Gaylord Hauser, and the brownies were her fist in the air to the guru of Hollywood health.

By the time I got home from school, Daddy usually would have returned home, often on the bus. The bus driver on that route never figured out that Daddy was blind until somebody told him, "You know, that Charlie Collins can't see, he's blind as a bat." Then the driver was embarrassed he hadn't noticed, although he was not alone, for it was my father's lifelong determination that no one should notice he was blind—not even himself. He wouldn't use a cane, and never used a Seeing Eye dog. He spent every energy to that end. He wore blue glass eyes that looked, to all the world, real. In the morning, struggling to get himself together for his day, he would occasionally drop one of those blue glass eyes on the tiles of the bathroom floor and it would crack, split, fly in a million pieces across the white riddle of stone. He had more; he was never at a loss for other eyes. The custom glass eyes came in little crates, like sets of eggs, from the factory near Denver where they were handblown and handpainted. They were perfect for my father, and if you didn't know he was blind, it would take you a while to guess, if you caught on at all. Probably only if you saw him drunk would you guess.

When the bus driver found out Daddy couldn't see, he offered him the lower price for people with disabilities. My father refused, saying he would pay the full price, just like everybody else. He was like that.

My memory of him is filled with the beauty of the songs he sang and the poetry that poured out of his ideas and his vision. On nights when he had a crowd around the Baldwin grand piano and on the radio in his morning shows, he would sing the great songs of Rogers and Hart and Gershwin, and if the mood was nostalgic and the hour late, he might do his rendition of Don Blanding's great poem, *Vagabond House*.

When I have a house . . . as I sometime may . . .
I'll suit my fancy in every way.
I'll fill it with things that have caught me eye,
In drifting from Iceland to Molokai . . .

As he recited the poem, he played resounding piano chords in the background, and when he had reached the final lines, ". . . Well . . . it's just a dream house, anyway," there was seldom a dry eye in the room. Daddy was an entertainer, and singer extraordinaire.

And he was a wonderful father. He loved his home and his children. Returning from a morning of music on the radio, Daddy would spend the afternoons doing chores for Mother, mowing the lawn with his feet bare so that he could "feel" where the lawn mower had been, practicing the piano, and collecting ideas and literature, jokes and songs, for his daily radio show. Then, when I had come home from school, before I started my own practice session at the piano, he liked to read aloud to me or to be read to from *Time* magazine or the "great books," Dostoyevsky, Melville, Dickens. He loved the afternoons with his children. I was the oldest.

He had struggled to live, to give his children good lives. He found it hard to understand why anyone would take his own life, when he had fought so hard to live his.

Al Taylor's death was haunting to my father, as it was to me, even as a ten-year-old. I learned from Al Taylor's daughter Hadley, later my sister-in-law, what happened on the night of Al's death. Hadley remembers the night of her father's suicide as being filled with unusual good humor. Al had dinner with his wife and family. His children, Gary, Peter, and Hadley, and his wife, Margaret, were in especially good moods. Hadley remembers they all made popcorn balls, sticking them together with caramel sauce, giggling and laughing at the mess, and smacking their lips over the sweet taste. Everyone was happy, and Al, who would soon be dead, was laughing. Then he went to the garage and turned on the ignition of his car. Later that night his wife, Margaret, discovered his body.

We didn't know that Daddy's depressions were probably caused by his drinking. Al Taylor had apparently been a heavy drinker as well, and suffered from depression like my father. We didn't know then that depression was an illness, like alcoholism. For my father, the nights of inebriation and the days of remorse that followed were his personal battlefield, and he fought like a tiger, like a man possessed, to regain his joyful, optimistic, cheerful moods again. He might have wondered, hearing the story of the suicide of a man who was really a stranger but whose life had already intertwined with people who were now his new friends, whether suicide might be in his own future, as well. It had come too close to his life for him to ignore. He would not live to know how very close.

In years to come, a then perfect stranger's desperate act would reverberate in my imagination. The death of a stranger came to mean more than an afternoon's chilling story. It became the background story to my own, and haunts me to this day, for in later years I would come to know Al Taylor more intimately than would ever seem plausible. His son Peter would become my husband and the father of my son, whose death by his own hand has driven me to this search for answers. His daughter Hadley, barely an acquaintance when I was ten, would become my close, lifetime friend, even after my divorce from her brother. Hadley had been six or so when her father died. At first, she was told he had gone on a trip. Later, when she learned her father had taken his life, she was shocked and bewildered. The true manner of Al Taylor's death had been kept a secret.

When I was in my twenties, my mother-in-law, Margaret, was helping me look through an old box of photographs of Peter. Among the pictures of this handsome man, my husband, as a little boy, we suddenly came to a picture of another handsome, smiling man, standing alone amid flowers with what looked like a pine tree behind him. My mother-in-law muttered an oath and ripped the photograph to shreds. By that time, I had discovered that her husband's suicide was buried along with all discussion of this sad, tragic man. No one in the family spoke of the reasons for his death or discussed what he had been like as a father, what kind of a person he was. I had been exposed to what I would come to know is the normal secrecy that surrounds suicide. It was a terrible secret to know.

In *Moby-Dick*, Melville wrote:

> *Whenever I find myself growing grim about the mouth; whenever it is a damp, drizzly November in my soul . . . I account it high time to get to sea as soon as I can. This is my substitute for pistol and ball . . .*

Time to read Melville's classic again, time to refresh my heart with the whales, the sea, the breadth of inspiration, the obsession of Ahab, the survival story that teaches its own lesson of courage and luck.

I wonder if my father ever knew that Melville's son committed suicide.

Like my father searching for reasons, like Melville with his substitute for pistol and ball, my heart is linked to the call of my own sea, the call to action—antidote to the call of depression, the alternative to suicide.

CHAPTER 2

Suicide—A Permanent Solution *to a* Temporary Problem

Almost Lost

*And the almond tree shall flourish . . . because man goeth
to his long home; . . . or ever the silver cord be loosed
Then shall the dust return to the earth as it was,
and the spirit shall return to God who gave it.*

—ECCLESIASTES

JOURNAL ENTRY, JANUARY 15, 1993

It has been a year today since you died, taking yourself from us, your spirit spinning into space, wandering into eternity where Gods and Goddesses surely caught you in their threads of light, easing your soul as it sped toward heaven, showing you the way at last. They bore your pain away and brought it down to me.

Today, the anniversary of your death, the very hour, we gather at the church with the priest who christened you, your family and your friends, the light from the rose windows shudders and glints with the words that are spoken to the thundering song of the bagpipes—"Amazing Grace, how sweet the sound, that saved a wretch like me"—the face of the bagpipe player, dressed in his plaid McClean kilts, is even younger than yours, even smoother than your smooth face; the voices of your friends and your family bring you to life in the echoing shadows and flames of the candles; you as a child, you as a man, you as a lover, you as a son, you as a friend; the flowers, white and amethyst, the glass, emerald and blue, the very sight, harp music in the air, where you were christened. You are there with us, your brightness and your beauty and your courage around us; I feel your face against mine like the wings of angels, my tears falling on the marble floor inlaid with colored slabs of stone. Though you are gone, yet you break the veil, the almond tree blossoms, you transcend time, you are with us, smile and laughter and brilliance and beauty and courage, ever irreplaceable, ever my child, ever my son, forever my teacher.

Bard of My Heart

I know I will find you among the bright flowers
We'll walk in the rain and we'll dance in the wind
We'll build a green bower and fish all the rivers
We'll watch the stars fall and we'll smile once again.
— JUDY COLLINS

By the time I was fourteen, I was playing quite a handful of piano. My parents made sure I had wonderful teachers; they probably spent more than they had on my musical education. By then I had been studying for years with Dr. Antonia Brico, a renowned teacher and internationally known conductor. I had made my successful debut with her orchestra in Denver, playing a Mozart two-piano concerto with another young pianist, Danny Guerrero. My parents were happy with my success, in school and in my piano practice. For most of my previous years, I had to come home and practice every day, including weekends. That year, I was learning a new piano piece called *La Campenella*, by Liszt, a real challenge. It was an extremely difficult piece of music, terribly hard. I was having trouble even committing it to memory in the manner taught by Dr. Brico. In her method, we did not hear the piece at all but memorized by analysis, studying each measure, finding the links between one set of quarter notes and the next, committing each page to memory. For me it was slow going. Every day after school I came home and tackled it, surrounded by my large family of three brothers, my mother and father, the bird and the dog, Koko.

My father was dazzled by the Liszt and would come home from a day of doing his radio show and listen to me play. He said he greatly admired the way my fingers flew over the keys, for the Liszt was a very impressive piece, flashy and grand. My father's eyes would close and he would listen, running his fingers through his hair and nodding his head from side to side, his sign of total approval, something we children longed to see, those times when he was sober and surrendered, and enjoying his life as the parent of four, soon to be five, when he took us in, and listened to us. When he saw us.

After practicing, I would help my mother with dinner, mindful that she was pregnant and hoping the new baby would be a girl, to go with my three brothers whom I loved and cherished. One night at dinner Daddy said that he wanted me to get *La Campenella* ready to perform at an appearance he was making at the Auto Show in Denver. I knew the Liszt was much too hard to have ready in the month before the Auto Show, but I didn't want to say no to him. I didn't want to disappoint him, or disobey him. I began, over the next month, to feel a terrible, dark, deep pain in my gut, in my soul, because I was trying to do something for my father that was beyond my talents, and beyond my abilities.

By then I had started to have a social life. I had my first date with Dave Larson. We went to the movies and necked in the back row, while on the screen Van Johnson stormed Omaha Beach and kissed a WAC dressed in starched linen. I didn't tell my parents about the kissing, just the Van Johnson parts. When Daddy and my mother went to the movies, I knew she whispered the visual story to him while he listened to the sound and nodded his head in that way he did, the way he nodded his head when I read him *Time* magazine every week, or shook his head in that way he did and pounded his fist into the armrest of the couch—swearing about McCarthy, about the French in Indo-China, about capital punishment, which he abhorred, about racism, for which he had no understanding, he said, because he wouldn't know what color you were, anyway.

But every day I played the Liszt, I alternated it with the Little Red Riding Hood music I was composing for my friends Carol and Marsha, Susan and Peggy for the High School Show, which was coming up. I told the story and played the piano for the sketch. But my father was not interested in Red Riding Hood. He was interested in the Liszt.

A month went by, and the Auto Show loomed closer as I practiced every day, knowing I would not be ready to perform *La Campenella* in public. One Saturday I was ironing, and my family, for some reason, was not present. Usually there was a full house at my home, Denver, David, Michael, and Mother pregnant with the wonder person who would turn out to be Holly. I was thinking about the Liszt, and ironing the shirts and the sheets. I did that; it was my job, the shirts and the sheets. I thought about the fingerings of the Liszt, which Dr. Brico had written in pencil under each note of the complicated piece. By now I knew I was going to have to say something to my father about the situation I was in. I knew I couldn't play the piece, but I also knew that I couldn't say no to him.

I had become terribly depressed, a condition that had been growing worse every day for the preceding month during which I was trying to finish memorizing the piece and bring the playing up to speed.

Suddenly that day, out of the blue, as they say, I thought about suicide, not as the plot in a novel and not as the solution taken by a stranger, but as the only way out. I thought about my death. It would be easy. I would take a bottle of aspirin; that would do it. I was sure of this, because we didn't take any other drugs, and aspirin was only doled out a few at a time when one of us children was very sick. Enough aspirin would kill me, I was sure. Enough would do the trick, say a hundred or so, and I would take enough.

I did not write a suicide note. They were smart enough, I

said to myself, to figure it out. They would miss me, and they would cry, and they would regret that they had not dealt with me more justly. That would be more just than a note. Anybody, I thought, could write a note. In my family, we were used to reading each other's minds, anyway.

I went to the bathroom and got out a full, unopened bottle—the economy size. I put it on the ironing board and got a glass of water and began to take the aspirin, fistfuls at a time. I would iron for a while, then cry and think how sorry they would be (They? My father, mostly) and how my funeral might look, and how my classmates would miss me, mostly Carol and Marsha, and how would they do the performance of *Little Red Riding Hood* without me? Peggy, the Woodchopper, and Susan, the grandmother, and Carol, the Wolf, and Marsha, Little Red Riding Hood. She was the most professional of my friends, studying dance in the way that I studied music, going two or three times a week for lessons, dancing in recitals and with her corps de ballet in her teacher's class. She would, when we were two years older, be chosen to go to England to study with the Sadler's Wells Ballet Company and would miss our junior year of school together. Her father was a well-known physician in Denver, and her mother was a friend of the family, as well. It occurred to me that Marsha would probably not be here in front of the ironing board, taking handfuls of aspirin with gulps of water. Marsha and my other friends were normal. It must have slipped into my mind that I was not. Our family did not seem normal. It seemed, always, frantic, and gifted, and erratic, and different. Very different. No one else had a blind father, that I knew of, and Roger Wilkowski, who lived over on Seventeenth

Street and whose father tuned pianos and was blind, like my father, was someone I would not meet until I was a senior in high school.

And so I ironed, and took thirty or so aspirin every few minutes, until I had consumed the entire bottle. My head was swimming, I thought it was tears. I didn't know what it felt like to die. Was I dying? I felt terribly sad, very alone, and the empty house was unusually still. Even my bird, Chris, who usually chirped and called my name, flying down the hallway to land on my head, chattering to me about many things while I did the ironing, or cleaned the dishes, singing while the water ran in the sink, was quiet, sitting somewhere in his cage, perhaps. The dog, Koko, was quiet. He was a cocker spaniel with soft, golden hair and long, soft ears. The bird, Chris, liked to ride on Koko's head, and Koko reluctantly allowed himself to perform this coach service, knowing he would be punished if he turned to bite at the blue-feathered creature who sang on his head, near his long ears, as though riding in a maharaja's carriage.

All was silent in the house as I was sure death was creeping on me. I became too weak to iron, sat down, and put my head in my hands. Lace curtains were drawn back against the kitchen windows, revealing the driveway next to our white stucco house. On a shelf above the kitchen sink, the set of blue, green, gold, and red aluminum glasses stood in rows. My mother got one each time she filled the Buick with gas. There were linoleum squares on the kitchen floor, pale green and brown, alternating colors. The squares began to swim before my eyes. I smelled the scent of starch, the soft fragrance of bread that Mother had baked that morning, the scent of the Russian olive tree outside the windows. It was spring, I remember, and outside in the garden there were flowers my mother coaxed up from the soil when she had two minutes, which wasn't often. There were tulips, red and orange. And buds on the trees. Where was everyone? Here I was, dying, and there was no one else around.

I slowly became aware of feeling sick to my stomach and knew I was going to throw up. I was sure death meant the end of feeling pain but I could not tolerate being sick to my stomach. I knew I was going to vomit. I knew that if being sick were part of the deal, I didn't want the rest of it, the dying part, either.

Even in those long-ago days, the telephone was my lifeline, our secret escape out of my friends' and my homes, into each other's presence. I dialed my friend Marsha's phone number, which I knew by heart. I called, and Marsha's mother, the wife of the doctor, Sherman, answered. I told her what I had done. She told me to put my head over the toilet bowl and try to make myself throw up. I knew she would know the answer. I told her I would, and she said Sherman would be right there. When my mother came home I was still throwing up. Dr. Pinto arrived and there were wet washcloths and soothing words from my best friend's father, the doctor.

My mother told me recently that when she was in the hospital, giving birth to me, she was reading *The Grapes of Wrath.* I told her that must have been the problem all along! She and I get along very well. We have a comfortable, easy, and totally frank relationship. I admire her so much, her energy and her intelligence. She is eighty-five this year, and has just read *Remembrance of Things Past,* with her book club. Her volunteer work includes twenty-five years at the shop at the Denver Art Museum, where she has been awarded and lauded for her service. She is close to all her children, and was very close to Clark, her first grandchild.

She was at the window of the delivery room watching, when he was born, at the Seventh-Day Adventist Hospital in Boulder. She loved Clark so much, and was devastated by his death.

The day after my episode with the aspirin, my father wrote me a letter in which he said he was sorry that he demanded so much of himself, and of his children, and admitted to being a perfectionist. He wrote that he was sorry I had taken this terrible step in reaction to his demands, which he understood that I couldn't fill. Please, he begged, forgive me, and don't do this again.

I began drinking a year after my suicide attempt, when I was fifteen. And from my first real drunk, in the back of a Hudson Duster on the road from Colorado Springs to Denver, where I held on to the gin bottle and threw up out the window, I accepted throwing up as part of the price of getting drunk and out of my pain. Whether I was trying to kill myself with pills, or drink myself to death, it was part of the deal. I knew that there was something in me that needed the drink—that medication, that tranquilization, and I knew, from the way I drank and the way my father drank, that I, too, was an alcoholic, although we never used that word in the family.

Growing up, we did not describe the elephant, we simply walked around it. Or ran around it. I knew that feeling I had in my stomach, that thing of being different from others, from Marsha with her ballet shoes and stage makeup, and Carol with her dedication to becoming a therapist, was very real. Like a demon in my soul, it could lead me to the dark place where I would try again to kill myself.

Before I turned sixteen, I started dating my husband-to-be, Peter Taylor, who would become the father of my son. You would not have known that I had a problem with alcohol, that is, if you didn't know the symptoms of the disease. Perhaps combined with my earlier attempt to take my own life, there were already signs that I was not as tightly wrapped as I might be. But I was an artist, a musician, a rebel, and it seemed that all of these habits—drinking, trying to kill myself, feeling as though the hole in my life was a part of my anatomy—were something like having auburn hair, or blue eyes. They were part of who I was, of who I am. No danger signs, just life as usual.

At times in my early twenties, the old fear that had caused me to try to take my life would come over me like a crawling, poisoning fog. I started to notice my drinking. Others started to notice it, although I wasn't a falling-down drunk, just someone who needed to drink more than others. I would be in a panic if I was sitting with you over dinner and the drinks had been served and my glass sat empty and it was too soon to order another without your taking note. Jung has said that these behaviors—smoking, drinking, avoiding, not being able to achieve an intimacy with others—point to an unconscious suicidal urge, or, it may be, to a "fatal resistance to life in this world."

Recently, I found a little set of ideas about drinking that seems to me to tell it all:

How soon we forget . . .

We drank for joy and became miserable.
We drank to be sociable and became argumentative.

We drank to feel sophisticated and became obnoxious.
We drank for friendship and made enemies.
We drank to help us sleep and woke up exhausted.
We drank to feel strong and it made us weaker.
We drank for exhilaration and ended up depressed.
We drank for medical reasons and acquired health problems.
We drank to help us calm down, and ended up with
    the shakes.
We drank to gain confidence and became afraid.
We drank to make conversation flow more easily and the
    words came out slurred.
We drank to lessen our problems and saw them multiply.
We drank to feel heavenly and felt like hell.

—ANONYMOUS

Life on life's terms was not to be easy. I came to learn that few people find it easy.

CHAPTER 3

Logan Lodge Memory

The hand that veils the future is the hand of God;
He can bring order out of chaos, good out of evil
and peace out of turmoil.

—*TWENTY-FOUR HOURS A DAY*

JOURNAL ENTRY, JUNE 1997

I was eating dinner with my friend Marsha from high school. I hadn't seen her for about eight years. Her voice sounds like her mother's voice, and like her own voice when she was a girl. She was a great and beautiful dancer, and I longed to fly as she did through the air, into the arms of men dancers, dressed in white gauzy filigree, on toe, wearing makeup.

"Do you have this feeling that I have, that no time has gone by?" I asked her. She smiled and nodded, and her laugh was like her mother's. Suddenly all of what we call time was not in the room. We were together in high school, before trouble, yet the time had not really passed, we were as young as we were then, for a moment.

When I was seventeen, I set out to work in the mountains. I had convinced my father to buy me a guitar, eased the strong ties with my piano teacher and the daily practicing, began spending time with others singers, learning songs, drinking beer, laughing, telling stories, being a teenager, having a life that was more about socializing and singing, and less about that strict discipline that had ruled my earlier life. I had found my true vocation. I was high on life, eager for what was coming next, and thrilled to be on my own for the summer, living in the mountains, working, paying my own way, as I would for the rest of my life.

I went to work at Grand Lake, in the magnificent mountains outside of Denver. I had a job in a lodge on a pine-forested point of land that stuck out into Grand Lake at the mouth of the Colorado River. I cleaned cabins, cooked meals, ironed, baby-sat, and did all the things teenagers do when they have summer jobs in the mountains; I was a jill-of-all-trades. At night I slept in a screened-in loft where I could hear and smell the rain, falling as it often does in the summer in the mountains, sweet and full of the scent of ozone and cedar, drifting even under the eaves of the pine loft. During those rainy afternoons, the lake pitted with raindrops, I stared up at the windows.

Georgia Logan was my boss. She owned and ran the lodge. And Georgia was a woman of few words. A few times a week, I pressed sheets between the steel plates of the ironing press, the steam rising up smelling of snowy cotton. This was my first summer at Logan Lodge.

The lodge and the cabins had been built sometime in 1930, part of the WPA, and probably housed the railroad workers who flooded into the mountains, on tracks flowing from Denver across the Continental Divide, out to the West Coast. The cabins were constructed of pine logs, and thirteen of them sat right up along the water of the little Colorado inlet. Logan Lodge was on the point, like the pointed end of a piece of pie. At its tip the Colorado ran out into Grand Lake, and anywhere on the property you could always hear the sound of the little Colorado running. I loved to work those cabins with the river moving along beside me, singing something like a refrain of the big song it sings when it widens out and cuts through the Grand Canyon. There was a set of rickety stairs in each cabin. Soon after I started working at Logans, all the catfish died and lay in the sparkling inlet with their bellies up and white, slowing down the inlet's flow. The ecologist fellows from Rocky Mountain National Park came in hip boots and big nets to scoop them out of the river.

The previous years I had worked at Sportsman's Valley Guest Ranch, where the owners, Hortense and Preston Beaver, who were Christian Scientists, were the exact opposite of Georgia Logan, talkative, customer oriented, and always full of a bright, positive, Mary Baker Eddy lightness that was contagious. They were tough, though, and had not wanted me back, the reason being, I assumed, that I had spilled coffee down a guest's shirt while serving breakfast and was the possibly the most erratic cabin cleaner of all the dozen girls they employed from around the country. So I was grateful to have the job at Logan.

I had a guitar by then, and wasn't wedded to the piano, practicing every day. Georgia had said in her letter that she had two kids. She and I would do the work together. That meant the thirteen cabins along the Colorado, and some light cooking for the immediate family, and the laundry. I could handle that, I thought. No breakfasts to serve, no coffee to spill down some greenhorn's shirt! A good-looking guy named Don drove onto the property every other day with the laundry truck. He would stop to pick up the big bags of laundry, and I smoked his Pall Mall unfiltered cigarettes from the red and white package. Cute guy, but I remember the taste of the cigarettes better than his face. The cigarettes made me dizzy since I didn't smoke them all the time, just when he, or someone else, offered. I wasn't buying yet.

The day before had been rainy and dreary. Nothing like a rainy August afternoon in the mountains. The tall pines dripped and the clouds hung over the lake. You couldn't water-ski, and you couldn't sit in the sun after the cabins were cleaned, and Georgia and the kids and I really had cabin fever, cooped up in the main house together. The rain had gotten to Georgia, and she had taken both kids and gone into town, leaving me with the ironing. I was in the kitchen of the main house about three in the afternoon when Ralph Wilton (which is not his real name), the father of a boy I knew from high school, came dripping and stamping through the screen door from the porch, with his fishing hat soaked and water running down his face. I was alone, and feeling very sorry for myself about the shirts, and the rain, and the fact that I didn't have any cigarettes. Mr. Wilton slammed the screen behind him and stood there, looking at me for a minute and then said; "You better call a doctor, I think my wife is sick."

The Wiltons had been at the lodge three days, getting away from Denver and the heat. He was a stationery man with a shop in Denver, which I used to pass on my way to my piano lessons. It smelled of pipe tobacco and rubber bands. He sold get well cards and birthday cards and hard candies and glass balls that had snow scenes in them. The Wiltons' only son, Carl, was a year ahead of me in high school. He was a blond, tall, athletic fellow who played on the football team, and whose arms bulged with great rippling muscles under his sports sweats. I used to watch him from afar at lunch, laughing with the girls who twirled the pom-poms, swaggering down the halls of East High. He was a great-looking, popular fellow. It made me nervous to be around him, his body seemed to ooze what I would later understand was testosterone. My father drank, and I knew after Carl's mother and father had been at Logan only a few hours that his mother drank, too. *Really* drank. I had seen bottles of sleeping pills and drugs in the bathroom cabinet when I cleaned their cabin, and there was the dogged look on Ralph's face all the time. He didn't get really drunk or giddy like his wife did but had a sorrowful, beat expression on his face.

He stood there, rain running down his clothes, making puddles around his fishing boots. He said I should call a doctor, that his wife wouldn't wake up. I went to the phone then and dialed the number. I told Doc Frazer's nurse she needed to come over to Logan's pronto and bring a stomach pump. Then I put on a rain slicker and followed Mr. Wilton back out into the rain and across the way to his cabin by the river. He said she was in bed, upstairs, and we climbed to the second floor on the rickety, switchback staircase.

I knew she was dead. She was wrapped up in a dark brown blanket with her arms around the pillow. There wasn't any note around anywhere, but I knew there must have been and I knew Mr. Wilton had taken it. I had never seen anyone dead before. I smiled, and did all I could do to keep from laughing out loud. The laughter crept up into my throat and I kept choking on it as I stood there, but I knew I had to look efficient, like I knew something to do about it or he would send me away, and I didn't want to be there, but I didn't want him to tell me to leave.

"We have to take off those rings," I said. Mr. Wilton looked at me funny. "You don't know who's gonna be up there at the morgue, you don't want anyone to snatch those rings, do you?" If he thought I didn't know she was dead before, he knew it now. Neither of us made any move to touch her, to give artificial respiration. She was cold and white, and as still as death can be. No stomach pump was going to be any good. Her pretty, pale face was strained. Her eyes were shut. Her fingers were stiff and it was hard getting the rings off. The wedding ring came off, finally, but one silver ring on her left little finger stuck right where it was, with the turquoise stone in it. Her hands were stiff, and I wondered now how long she had really been dead, and to this day I don't remember anything unusual about her body. There was no smell, just the scent of her shampoo, or maybe it was her perfume. They say people lose control of their bodily functions when they die. Maybe that only happens when you are stabbed or shot or hanged. But there was none of that, or maybe he had cleaned her up. There was only the smell of the pine logs and the sound of the little inlet mummering its way into the lake.

I heard the station wagon pull up outside the cabin, and the screen door slammed, just once, so I knew Doc Frazer wasn't back and it was only his nurse and there would only be three of us to get her down that narrow stairway. Like a mountain switchback, the staircase came up away from the ground floor and then doubled in on itself for the next few steps. Mr. Wilton was big enough so he barely squeezed through the turn. I didn't know how we were going to get her around that hairpin curve on her way out of here.

"We're up here, up the stairs."

"She's here, upstairs."

Mr. Wilton and I said all the words together from the upper floor. Doc Frazer's nurse climbed up the stairs to where we waited. She was dressed in her uniform, with a blue sweater pulled over her shoulders.

"My God," was all she said. She went over and put her ear down over Mrs. Wilton's face and her fingers over her wrist and looked at me when I smiled. I still had a wide grin on my face that wouldn't peel off, or shut down. I had tried to think of something awful to get my mind off smiling but nothing would come. I thought of losing my bird, Chris, I thought about the time my brother Dave came home with blood running out of his white hair into his eyes and down his face when somebody dropped a bucket on his head. But nothing seemed to bring me to my senses. I just kept grinning.

We three stood there. I looked at Mr. Wilton. I figured she took a lot of pills the night before, when she was very drunk, pulling at that bourbon all night, sweating and then swaggering in front of the fireplace, telling me stories of her life in Denver, where she was quite a society woman, to hear her talk. They had only been there a few days, but they did the same things all three days. They would come down to the lodge and sit around our fire after eating dinner in town—we didn't serve meals to the guests, but I cooked most of the ones for Georgia, the kids, and myself—they had their own liquor and would pour it out into the glasses I brought in from the kitchen, and fill the glasses up with ice, but no water. He didn't drink much, just let his drink sit, letting the ice melt.

The night before, she and Mr. Wilton began to argue in nasty and mean voices that sent the children out of the room, to their mother's shooing hand. It got ugly and then they left, Mr. Wilton guiding his wife out the screen door and along the river's edge to their cabin. She could hardly stand. I could still hear them fighting, everyone could, she shouting loud, berating him all the way to the cabin, and he arguing back, but softer, trying to get her into the cabin, out of hearing. I didn't really know what the argument was about, but it seemed to be that she was drinking too much and that he had some kind of difficulty with his business. She kept saying, I hate you, I hate you. He had smiled at us at first and then began to try to shush her up.

And then I had seen all the pills in the cabinet in the bathroom. Sleeping pills, mostly. As I made my way down the stairs carrying Mrs. Wilton in the dusky blanket like a sack of potatoes, she didn't feel like potatoes. She felt like, what? She was so stiff we had to bend her to get her around that corner, and I know she creaked and resisted our pushing her arms and legs around inside the blanket. Rigor mortis, I remember thinking. Rigorously dead. "Muscular stiffening following death" is what the dictionary says. Well she had it.

We did manage to shove her around the twist in the stair-case, and while the three of us held her various elbows and legs up, I heard another car pull up. The screen door slammed again, and Doc asked us what we were doing. It was still raining out-side, so he was dripping on the braided rug upstairs and stood looking at a laughing girl, a man in a fishing hat, and his own nurse hauling what looked like a bag of soup bones across a room. I had covered up Mrs. Wilton's face because I thought that was what you did, and neither the nurse nor Mr. Wilton had pulled the blanket away.

"She's dead and I thought I better bring her over to the of-fice for you to look at." Doc nodded at his nurse and looked over the blanket at me. "She's having hysterics, can't you see that?" he said. I couldn't get my lips to stay over my teeth and I didn't know what to say, so I said, "Georgia had to go to Grandby. She'll be back at six. She'll be mad. "

You know, Georgia Logan *was* mad at me. She was a funny woman. Now that I'm her age, I think I can understand why she was so tight-lipped. She had had a husband I romantically envi-sioned as handsome, who had been killed in some strange acci-dent in Kansas twelve years before. Georgia got a lot of money from the insurance, due to the peculiar nature of his death, and she decided fresh air and Colorado sunshine would work out the kinks for her and the two kids. Pat's foot was badly crippled from polio, but he got around okay. Cindy was good at washing dishes and just about nothing else, but she was sweet. So Georgia bought the lodge and made a go of it, barely, every summer. She didn't make a fortune, but she stayed a little ahead and she knew the pie-shaped corner on the Colorado and Grand Lake was gonna be worth a mint some day. This was her fifth season and her first suicide. No wonder she was mad at me.

Ron Cook came over that night after they took Mrs. Wilton away. He came in the front room, slamming the screen door behind him.

"I heard that some woman who was staying here died this afternoon, a suicide." It was not a question. Ron was very tall under a full-sized Stetson, very brown and handsome. His mother, Ruth, was a friend of Georgia's and was married to a man who was a big rancher up the valley. He was divorcing Ruth. She used to come over to Grand Lake to talk her troubles over with Georgia, and I overheard, over many glasses of whiskey, most of the story of her life and troubles. Because I was usually around at night, cooking dinner or cleaning up, she would talk with me, too. At me, really. Ron had been flirting with me most of the summer. Peter, with whom I had a serious romance by that time, and to whom I wrote long, loving letters most weeks, and from whom I got wonderful letters as well, was a Naval Air Cadet stationed in the south. I hadn't seen him in months. I appreciated being flirted with.

"Where were you for the last couple days?" I said to Ron. "Never mind somebody died here, only excitement brings you around."

"I went to Denver to sell some cattle for my father," he said. Georgia and Ruth came into the room with drinks in their hands.

"Go get a beer, Ronny, and quit standing there with your hat on." She had a glass of bourbon in her hands, and Georgia had a coke. Georgia didn't, or couldn't, drink. It was a relief. "Hello, honey," Ruth said to me. "Ain't he handsome, that son of mine?" Ron had gone into the kitchen, but he heard her. "He wouldn't let me take an overdose of pills, would you, hon?" she shouted after him. Georgia gripped her glass and looked at me. We had talked about Mrs. Wilton's death a little before dinner, and she had told me not to discuss it at all with anyone. Georgia was a woman of few words, except when she was around drinkers, and then they got fewer. She must have used a few of her well-chosen words to let Ruth know what had happened. Ruth had seen the Wiltons drinking three nights before; in fact, all of them had gotten pretty drunk together. I didn't say anything.

"I got problems enough," Ruth went on, taking a huge swig of neat scotch, the good stuff, Johnnie Walker Black Label. She didn't blink as it went down, but wiped her sleeve on her mink coat. Against all reason, Ruth wore the long, pale mink here in the mountains, over her jeans or over nothing. "I think she might have done the right thing. Thing I'd do if I had the guts, fellas." Ruth always called us fellas, me and the kids and Georgia.

The kids were crouched in front of the fireplace, reading, or pretending to read. "Do you think I'm happy in my mink?" Come to think of it, Ruth always reminded me of Mae West. She was big and blond and loud and thought she was funny. "That bastard bought this for me nine years ago," she said, stroking the fur of her coat, "when he still thought I was the cutest thing since Wear Ever spark plugs. It's a beauty, don't you think?"

Ron came back into the room, hugging his glass mug of beer, looking into the fireplace. I had pulled the screen over the grate after poking at it a while to get the flames going good and my face was hot and I looked over at the mink coat sprawled across the sofa by the door. I didn't like mink and I still felt shaky about everything and I wished Ron and his mother had not come by at all.

"Do you know how I knew he was gonna divorce me? He held his secretary's coat out for her first when we were leaving a restaurant one night. A big seal coat, brand new. And I knew." Ruth was going to be rich when the marriage was over. She was rich now. But I don't think she wanted it that way. She wanted to be the wife of her husband, the rancher.

"Ron's stepmother-to-be's a good lookin' woman, just a little bit older than my son. Ronnie, you always liked *older* women, didn't you, son?" She meandered into the kitchen and poured herself more Black Label, bringing the bottle back into the living room, where she took a seat near the fire and put the bottle on the table where she could reach it.

"Now, Georgia, this suicide thing." Georgia winced and looked at me. "My mother didn't approve of suicide, but it's all the rage now. Pills, booze, cars. I won't let Ronnie have a motorcycle, I don't think young people should be able to decide everything about their lives. Do you think all of us commit suicide, choose how we're going to die? I'm going to die of wealth, loaded down with jewels, smothered in stocks."

"Why did she take sleeping pills?" Ron said.

"She was a nice woman, very quiet, very nice," said Georgia. It was the first word out of her all evening. "I don't think we can assume she did any such thing, maybe she *did* have a heart attack." I thought, Georgia is almost waxing verbose, for her.

Upstairs in my room the night before, I had seen a huge moth hanging on the screen of my bedroom window. I had tried to shake it off the screen. It just hung there. I slapped the screen and it fluttered, but it still hung on. I was afraid of it but didn't want to kill it, so I turned out the light and got into bed and had nightmares all night.

"I think I knew someone was going to die last night," I said. "I saw a moth as big as an owl. It was spooky." It would have been about the time poor Mrs. Wilton was dropping the pills down her throat. I was sitting on the couch and Ron's legs were stretched out in front of me, pouring into a pair of hand-tooled Dustin boots.

"I'm sure a person gets lonely up here with only the moths for company, or Pat and Cindy and me." Georgia, I thought, I never knew you cared. The shock of death had loosened our tongues.

Ruth stood up from the couch, unsteady on her feet.

"Oh, Georgia, I would like to know how I'm supposed to go on like this, with an empty glass." She held the glass up to the fire and looked at it closely. "What was in here? Diesel fuel? Ronny, son, go out and get me another drink, and make it plain diesel fuel, no branch water, no ice. And take it easy on the beer—you're driving home."

"Do you suppose the police are going to come tomorrow?" Ron said when he came back into the room with his mother's drink. "I mean, if she didn't die of a heart attack. I mean, I suppose if they don't come you'll know it was a heart attack." I thought he must be drunk. The phone rang; it was my friend Marny Sorrenson. She said she was in town at a local bar and had heard the news of the suicide and was coming over. Georgia gave me a look. Marny worked down the road at another guest ranch, and was engaged to Lee Howard, a cowboy in the county. She and I had become friends through my boyfriend, Peter.

Ruth drank a lot more while we waited for Marny. It was getting late, and all I really wanted to do was to go to sleep, hoping the moth had flown the coop and was not sitting on my screen in the darkness. Marny came in the door about twenty minutes later. She came over and hugged me. "Are you all right?" she asked. I nodded. "I heard all about it. That's such a terrible way to die, all boozed up and hating your husband's guts. I know in the morning she would have changed her mind and gone for a hike, or water-skied." We all listened to the falling rain outside, which hadn't let up all day. "Maybe not water-skied, but you know what I mean. Gotten on with it."

Ron brought Marny a bottle of Coors. "I heard somewhere that every life ends in a dreadful execution," he said. "Did you ever try to kill yourself?" I had never told anyone about my suicide attempt, and would not for twenty years.

"I tried once, after a fight with Lee," Marny said. "Last year. But then, I just smashed up his truck. I ran it into that little gully right behind the ranch. Just rammed the gears and smashed in the front end, and felt stupid. He made me get it repaired myself, and pay for it."

"Lucky it wasn't mine, I'd have whupped your hide. A lady

should never wreck a man's pickup," Ron said, smiling at Marny. I always thought he was sweet on her.

"That wasn't a real suicide attempt, honey." Ruth was swirling the last of the bourbon around in her glass. She had her mink on now; signal it was time to go. "If you had died, it would have just been an accident."

"Sing us a song about love, Judy," Ron said. "Enough of this gloomy subject. You know the song about the seven brothers and the sister with the golden hair?" It was a sad, sweet song of death.

"That's a song about love, but it's about death, too," I said. "He dies in a quarrel over this long-haired woman."

"Oh damnation," said Ruth, squirming out of her chair, where she had sunk down again. "Let's hear a song, and then I'm gonna get this boy to drive me home, if he can still drive." She swayed across the room to the fireplace and put her glass down on the mantel. She sat down beside me. "Sing it, girl," she said.

I got to the sixth verse of the "Dewey Dens of Yarrow," where the lyric says:

Her hair it was three quarters long
And the color of it was yellow;
She wrapped it round his middle so small
And she carried him home from Yarrow.

Ruth shoved my shoulder hard, throwing me off balance. The guitar fell to the floor. "That's too sad," she said. "I want to hear something pretty, that we can dance to. You sing too many sad songs." Her breath was sour and she slurred her words.

I reached down and picked up the guitar and said, "I'm going to bed."

There was a long crack in my National Guitar, from the bottom, where the pegs sit next to the sound hole in the middle. When I got upstairs, I slammed the door to my bedroom and heard Ron's voice saying goodnight and the car doors slam. They were on their way home, mother and son, the drunk and the heir. I sat there on the bed and felt the crack in the guitar and listened to the rain dripping. Still raining. Marny's voice said, "Kid," and there was a knock. She came in and switched on the lamp by the bed. I was sitting there on the bed in the dark with the guitar in my lap.

"Will it be all right?"

"I guess it can be fixed. It's kinda like Lee's truck. Only I can't get Ruth to fix it. She doesn't know what she's doing, or what she's saying when she's like that."

"Why does Georgia let her drink so much when she comes here?"

"It's Ruth's bottle. And, well, she usually isn't so bad, just talks a lot and laughs a lot. She can usually drive home on her own; she's never brought Ron along to take her back. I think she knew she was gonna get ploughed when she came over here tonight. She's worried about the divorce, and maybe Mrs. Wilton's death was a sign for a real good time."

"Do you want to go for a walk?"

"It's raining, Marny."

"Put on your slicker and some galoshes, we'll walk down by the lake for a minute. It's nice in the rain, then I'll go back up to Angel's Hand. "

I got my gear and we went back down the stairs. The fire was nearly out and Georgia was sitting there, staring into what was left of it.

"You are both crazy. It's raining hard and it's late. Judy, you got to be up early, to start checkouts with me." I looked at her and she knew what I was asking. She shook her head. "I did the Becks' cabin already. But tomorrow's Monday."

"Thanks, Georgia. We won't be long."

"Ugh," said Mrs. Logan.

It was really raining hard and we squished through the pine needles on the ground in front of the house and squashed through the mud for a while till we got to the lawn, which stretched out to the edge of the lake. We watched the moon struggle to get through a little bit of clear sky, where the clouds were parted on the other side of the lake; then the moon ran back into the cloud bank, rain driving away the little bit of light. The trees were dripping water, the pine needles spools of silver, the swoosh of the wind driving the rain right out onto the lake.

"I'm freezing, Marny, and I've got to get to bed. Maybe I can sleep."

Georgia was still sitting in front of the fire, but it had gone completely out.

"The police called. They wanted to know did I find a bottle of pills in the cabin this afternoon?"

"They called tonight? My God, it's nearly midnight."

"Well, you know, it is still officially the day she died. I told them we'd look again, but we didn't see anything like that. Did you, Judy?" Georgia had said more tonight than she had said to me in the two months I had worked for her.

"No, Ma'am, but I think Mr. Wilton pretty much cleared the place out even before he came up here this afternoon. You know yourself there was a lot of stuff there yesterday morning in the bathroom cabinet. It was gone this afternoon after they took his wife away. He went back to Denver, you know."

"I'm all tuckered out and I'm going to bed, and you should too."

"'Night, Marny."

"'Night, Georgia," I said. The next day the papers in Denver said Mrs. Wilton's death had been due to a coronary failure. My folks called to find out about it. I told them I thought she had killed herself.

"I don't want you to come down here," my father said, "bad as you feel. You have a job up there and somebody dying in one of Georgia Logan's cabins doesn't change that one bit. What did Georgia say?"

"Oh, I suppose she expects me to stay. She paid me already this week." Georgia and I had our fights, and I was not the last word in dependability, so I kept thinking all summer she might fire me. But I had grown to like Georgia Logan, even to admire her. There were too many words in the world, and I was coming to appreciate her silences.

"But I feel so awful, it just makes me sick because I know Mr. Wilton knew she was up there all morning and practically all afternoon, and he waited so long to do something." I thought then, and I think now, that he had let her die. Letting her die, to me, was a worse crime than killing her outright.

"Well, honey, you don't know that. You just don't know what the man was doing, where he was, or anything about that."

But I knew I did. Poor man, I thought. Poor stationery man. And whatever the truth, he'll always know.

CHAPTER 4

Checkmate

Death of the Dream

The bustle in the house
The morning after death
Is solemnest of industries
Enacted upon Earth, —

The sweeping up the heart,
And putting love away
We shall not want to use again
Until Eternity.

—EMILY DICKINSON

JOURNAL ENTRY, JULY 7, 1992

In the days after my son's suicide, I moved in a fog, per-
forming the things that had to be done. The death notice went into the papers and came out not at all the way I

would have wanted it, for kind friends put the words together I could not speak or write. The notice told only the details, not the important things, not the things that wrench the heart, that should have been shouted from the cold, snow-covered rooftops of a winter-bound city. The notice could have said, My heart weeps, where are you, how could you leave? Your monuments of achievement are here in my heart, I told you when you were here on earth, but not as many times as I might, or you would have heard me, you would have stayed.

I had a dream a few nights ago. It is summer, a year and eight months after your death. I dream I have lung disease, my heartbeat is practically nonexistent. In the hospital I lie waiting to die. I think always of you, my son.

But after sleep, after dreams, there is daylight, and joy, and laughter. I am not complete, and yet I *am* complete, knowing the world has changed, knowing more of life through death.

Let me feel joy, feel love, feel closeness, with my friends, my family, knowing I have had much of heaven on earth.

Nowadays particularly, you see, the world hangs on a thin thread, and that is the psyche of man. We are the great danger. The psyche is the great danger. What if something goes wrong with the psyche?

—CARL JUNG

Clark. Beautiful. Red hair and blue eyes. Bright blue, like mountain rivers in sunlight, like the sky on a Colorado day, the snow reflecting the brilliance of the blue. A sense of humor as shining as his blue eyes, a smile that was never a smirk, never mean. He never made fun of another person's weaknesses. He got along well with people, made friends easily—the homeless man in the street, the most beautiful girl in the room, the poet, the Ph.D., the down-and-outer, the heiress, the dishwasher at the diner, the bipolar neighbor named Gene, who lived in the apartment under us and used to bang on his ceiling (our floor) with a baseball bat, screaming that the sound of the (imaginary) music was driving him mad. Clark said we had to love Gene, that he was our family, too.

Clark was born in the Seventh-Day Adventist Hospital in Boulder Colorado, on January 8, 1959. He was a gift, a magical, lyrical, beautiful spirit. My mother, along with Peter Taylor, my husband, watched Clark's birth through the window of the delivery room. It took me twenty-eight hours to deliver him. He weighed nine pounds and two ounces at his birth. He was healthy and strong, sweet and good-natured. He slept through the night at about six weeks. His father and I were proud parents, holding and fondling him, talking to him all the time. I sang to Clark and carried him around in my backpack when I hiked in the mountains of Colorado or the streets of Boulder, shopping, walking, and visiting. Our early years were kind and smiling. He thrived and grew, beautiful and happy.

Alongside candles on the birthday cakes, baby rattles and little white leather shoes, first-grade teachers and lollipops, camp clothes with Clark's name sewn on and first haircuts, first steps, first girlfriends, there was the family secret.

No one talked much about Al Taylor.

Clark was a happy baby, and a happy little boy, and a young man who was a charmer, who could study Chinese calligraphy and make a mean omelet, come up with flowers for me when it was winter and he had run out of money, and sit and talk to me for hours about a sunset he had seen or his half sister and her problems, and her beauty, or his high school homework. He read Krishnamurti when he was thirteen and talked about living clean and learning to meditate.

In later years, there was a sort of sadness in Clark, an aloneness, a differentness that reminds me, now that I think of it, of Bruce Coburn's lyric, "I never knew what you all wanted, so I gave you everything." I've always felt there was a way in which Clark never found his own boundaries, or his own peace.

Yet why should my son's life be defined by his manner of death? He was more than his death. He was his vibrant life, a life of stretches and flashes of brilliance, of deep joy, of a journey that found meaning and beauty in the world, with his friends, with his family. He had great gifts, not the least of which was an empathy with others that gave them hope and consolation. He could see around the rocks and boulders of human failings; he could see into the heart. He was a remarkably alive and growing young man, a success in his life, and a power of example for those who loved him and those who hardly knew him. Why should his life be defined in this moment of insanity that took him from me and from his family and friends? That is not justice, taking one moment that will last forever and holding it up against all the other moments in which he survived, in which he triumphed, in which his sweetness and his tender care for his child, for his family and friends, so that they are overshadowed by catastrophe.

Clark could be a delight, and he could be a handful. He was exposed to art and culture and music growing up. He responded eagerly to the arts, learning to sing and play the guitar, painting and drawing easily and early. He read at a young age, as his father and I both read to him and encouraged him to listen to stories and read books.

As he grew up, there were problems, some of them certainly arising from the fact that his father and I divorced, and there was a custody battle that probably set up large and unanswerable questions in Clark's mind. It is my belief that Clark's mental and emotional health were deeply affected by the judge's decision that I should not have custody of him. The battle for custody was long and hard, and the outcome difficult for both of us. He lived with his father when I lost custody and then came back to live with me. There were drugs and alcohol in Clark's life then, and although I didn't know what the problems were, I tried every way I could to help him. But by the time he was in his late teens, it was clear he had difficulties I could not solve, though I tried.

I was seeing a lot of therapists, and so was he, and why no one suggested a rehab for alcoholism is still beyond me. But Clark was young, and there was no understanding yet in the culture about rehabilitation and its power to change the lives of people addicted to drugs and alcohol. Hazelden, the mother of all rehabs, in Minnesota, had been open a few years. There were no movie stars going into treatment every other day and talking about it in the press. I was still drinking and a long way from treatment myself. It was like being gaslighted, on a dark street, with no signs to tell you where you were or where you might find help. My son and I just struggled to stay up with what life was handing both of us.

By the time he was sixteen, in 1975, Clark felt he had received the help he needed. After a year and a half, during which he was at a psychiatric hospital in Baltimore where we did a lot of therapy together and worked hard, he simply disappeared. Though he kept in touch with me, he would not tell me where he was for a few months.

In the spring of 1976, he came back to New York to live with me and finish high school. We made a deal. He would not drink and he would not use drugs.

All the while, I tried, seeking professional advice, going to counseling for me and for my son, stalking the dragon, following the clues, trying to find out what I could do to make Clark happy, to help him find himself.

Together, we looked over many schools, most of which accepted him and were only a few minutes away from where we lived. Clark chose a school in Brooklyn, Saint Ann's, which would be a long subway ride each way. But he and I both liked Saint Ann's, the teachers as well as the headmaster, who seemed to really get who Clark was—bright, eager, with a mixed bag of experience that was not a detriment, but an advantage. At Saint Ann's, Clark worked hard, got good grades, and made friends.

Clark always made friends. Like his father, Peter Taylor, and his father's friends, and his grandfather, Chuck, my dad, he loved to chew the fat, discuss philosophy and poetry, Eastern religion and cooking, rock and roll and, later, when he got sober, Dr. Bob and Bill W., cofounders of Alcoholics Anonymous. He would spend three hours talking to me about semiotics, convinced that if he just talked long enough about this exotic field (the study of signs and symbols in culture, a field that includes language, art, décor, architecture, couture, jewelry, and anything else that might be interpreted as carrying a signal to other tribes), I would certainly understand (I never did!). He would get totally obsessed with the guitar and play (and he played well, much better than I do) until his fingers were raw and his back ached from hunching over the instrument. He could recite William Blake's poetry, which was his father's field of study, and sing the songs of Crosby, Stills and Nash, and the traditional songs, which were mine. He didn't care very much for material things, an idea that was part of the philosophy of the rest of his family but probably also came from his own assessment that, at the heart of it, these things didn't mean very much.

He could make me laugh out loud and cry my heart out. He was beautiful on the outside, and on the inside, where it counted most. That was the beauty that everyone saw, that kindness and generosity of spirit that Clark had as a child, and continued to have as a man. I am proud of him now, as I was when he was alive. He was a truly special, gifted, tender man. He did me proud as a mother, and he always will.

There were a few more years of chaos, and a series of schools—Columbia, Saint Ann's, Rhode Island School of Design—and Clark got worse. I despaired of his ever really getting well.

But the night is darkest before dawn, and in 1984 the miracle happened and Clark decided that he wanted to live. He had what he would later call his spiritual awakening on the steps of The Cathedral Church of St. John the Divine in New York City, on the morning of February 13, 1984, at dawn. He called me, came for coffee, and told me that he had decided to go away to get clean. He got sober at Hazelden, in Minnesota, where his life, and mine, began all over again. I was also sober by then. In the happy years to follow, Clark married, had a beautiful child, and rebuilt his life. This was a time of joy and celebration. He was finally stable and healthy, and by 1991 had been sober for seven years, was married and the father of a baby girl whom he loved deeply. I thought my son Clark was really out of the woods, healthy, and happy, it seemed, and except for the problems of living, the ones we all have, I was sure he was going to make it.

I wanted Clark to be happy, no matter what he chose to do with his life, to figure out that he was responsible for making his life happy, and to find a passion of some kind that would make him shine and give him satisfaction. In the seven years before his death, he put a solid foundation under his feet and got fully into recovery.

After nearly seven years of sobriety, Clark relapsed and, in January of 1992, took his life. The last time Clark and I talked was five days before his death. My last words to him were "I love you, Clark." His last words to me were, "I love you, Mom."

Clark taught me to be a mother, first. He taught me that I could change and learn about motherhood, that motherhood is more than providing breakfast cereal and winter boots. He taught me that forgiveness is the greatest gift and that amends can be made and lives changed. He taught me that nothing is forever. And that everything is spirit.

Clark taught me many things, but his death by his own hand has been my greatest teacher. In the wake of his suicide, I have had to face my own demons, take stock of myself, send out all the green shoots of life that might have withered, and hold them in a fierce embrace against the stones and monuments of memory and the future. It has taught me to lock those shoots of green in the total grip of passion: my own passion for life.

I must always think of those wonderful, magical years with my son. No matter the years, the pain, the sorrow, there was joy, abundant, complete, reverberating through my life and the lives of everyone who knew him. Clark will always be my son.

And I will always be his mother.

Born to the Breed

I was only nineteen
The morning you were born
With your hair fine and red
And your eyes like my own

Barely a woman
With only a song
I sang to keep you smilin'
And held you all night long

Home through the streets
With you in my arms
Cold winter mornings
In a Colorado town

I've seen you stumble
You've watched me fall

You know I've got nothing
You know we've got it all

Rain comes down and the trucks rollin' by
Does that old parka keep you dry?
Sixteen years old, out on the road
Tryin' to get to the sky

Back in September
You call'd me on the phone
"Ma, you know I love you,
But I gotta be own my own
Comes a time in a boy's life
When he's got to be a man,
Please don't try to find me
Please try to understand."

Got me a job in a rock and roll band
Gonna try to see if I can get by
Sixteen years old, out on the road,
Tryin' to get to the sky.

I've watched you grow
Thru all these years
You've seen me stumble
I've watched your tears

Sometimes there were roses
Sometimes it was thorns

But I know you're gonna make it
As sure as you were born

And I hope from what you wanted
You get what you need
I know you're gonna make it
You were born to the breed

Sixteen years old
Out on the road,
Tryin' to get to the sky

—JUDY COLLINS

CHAPTER 5

Snow Angels *and* Stained Glass

*I tell you that the Spirit can overcome the sword and pain
and sorrow; the Spirit completely realized will guide and
protect you and lead you through all dangers; it will give
you strength, power and inward peace. This is the reward of
eternal vigilance, of the realization of Him as your
companion.*

—LETTERS OF THE SCATTERED BROTHERHOOD

JOURNAL ENTRY, APRIL 20, 1997

A closeness to the Spirit guides me and eases my heart
in meditation. You knew about this closeness to
God. Your abrupt departure does not change the fact that
you were and are a spiritual soul. You took the fast train
but I know you saw the scenery, I know you often saw
more than I did. You and I talked about spiritual things
easily, with no separation of images, no difficulties. We

discussed the constant fight to rise above the things that would pull us down.

I can transcend my pain and lose myself in the wonder of the Spirit. I know you are safe with that spirit and that I am guided, healed, and held in the place of light by the same Spirit that holds you safe.

When a crime has been committed, police and criminal investigators walk the grid of the crime scene, looking for clues. They go over the scene in a meticulous way, grasping at the tiniest clues, plucking feathers or hairs or fibers or miniscule traces of fabric and blood and perfume, even body lotion, hair spray, shoe sizes, footprints, fingerprints, dusting for powder, traces of dirt, anything to place the perpetrator in some kind of context, to find the answer to who did the dirty deed.

Suicide, a crime against oneself as well as others in one's life—the victims are guilty of everything, it seems—is always investigated by the police as though it may not be suicide, but murder. They walk the grid.

Ever since my son's death, in some way, I, too, have been walking the grid, looking at every fact about my son's death. It means reading everything I can get on suicide. (Not many articles or books were in print when he died. I found those that were helpful, and since 1992 there have been some very good ones written about suicide and depression.)

I know from walking that grid that anyone who saw the facts for what they were would have known that my son was on the veritable edge of completing the act of suicide for months before his death. He tried, and failed, and tried again.

I also know that although he blamed others for his mood of the day, no one is responsible for his death other than himself.

In my grid walking, my meticulous searching, I later read of a psychiatrist who took a suicidal patient through an exercise. He asked her to write her death note. When she couldn't come up with anything concrete, he helped her, wrote a note, folded it, and handed it across his desk. When she opened the note, she read, "Fuck you."

Suicide, though it may have many causes, is often the ultimate third finger salute, the clutched fingers under the chin, fist against the forearm, and curse to anyone near enough to get the message. Survivors of suicide are routinely implicated and may feel guilty. They tend in retrospect to check out everything they ever said or did with regard to the suicide. You hear it all the time—"He called, I didn't call him back. I feel so guilty!" "God, I didn't answer that letter, I should have answered that letter! I was going to, I just didn't have the time, and now, look at what has happened!" As though anything we might have done could have changed the outcome. "I should have known, I could have known, I might have, if I had only known, known!" "He looked so well, he was happy. I have never seen him so happy, he clicked his heels, he was so happy, how could I have known?" Of course, experts should have known. I have some friends whose son hanged himself in a tree on the grounds of the hospital in which he was being treated for suicidal tendencies. They searched, when he first died, to find out what they might have done to prevent his going out into the air, into the sun, with something that might serve as a tool for hanging—a sheet, I think it was. How I looked for clues everywhere. Alyson, Clark's widow, gave me journals of

Clark's, his notebooks, and even his song lyrics. I searched them as though hunting for a killer.

All survivors are suspect—in a way, everyone the suicide has ever met. The parents, of course, also wives, husbands, lovers, friends, teachers, and professionals who either tell the truth or don't. Because there are certain kinds of news none of us want to hear. "You are fine, you are going to live." What a statement! And here I thought I was in trouble and might have to do some other chores, other than getting up in the morning and getting on with life. I might have to learn to take certain pills, go to therapy for dying, sign a lot of papers, and check out my insurance myself! There was the hospital that treated Clark in the first attempt he made to kill himself. Why didn't they do more?

After Clark's death, I looked into bringing a malpractice suit against the hospitals where had been treated. His first hospitalization was after his initial attempt, three months before his death, and the second, two weeks before his death, at which time he was given an opportunity to write and reflect, talk and get professional consultation about his relapse and his previous suicide attempt. I felt the sorrow, let it roll over me and around me, let it boil up and claim me, let it wrench the tears out of my eyes and let it roll into rage.

At home in the months to come, there were cats to feed and teas to make and tears to shed and, somehow, there were dinners that got made, and eaten. I found it hard to eat as well as breathe, and ate meals as though they were my last and would lead me somewhere I could hide from having to breathe. Like death.

But I did not want to die. I wanted to live, just not like this. Some other way, where the outcome was different.

Later, after the shock had worn off, I raged, slamming things down on counters and throwing books across the room, hitting my fists against the walls, wanting my broken heart to break against some wall or some force that would draw blood from the bleeding heart that pounded under my chest.

There was snow outside. The temperature chill, so cold whole continents seemed locked in ice. At night when I fell into bed exhausted, I was sure, as I finally drifted into sleep at four and five and six in the morning, that I wouldn't live to see another day, or that I would wake from this nightmare to find it was just that, a nightmare. I prayed that when dawn came it would all be over, be not true, be anything but this. The lore of the survivor, never encountered, never dreamed of—for who would dare harbor such a dream in normal, everyday life?—began to take shape. I learned as much as I had to learn every day, to get through that day. No more than I could bear for that day. I survived, one day, one night, one prayer, one candle at a time. One breath at a time.

And with my own mantra:

Just for today, I will not take my life.

CHAPTER 6

You Might *as* Well Live

Resume

Razors pain you;
Rivers are damp;
Acids stain you;
And drugs cause cramp;
Guns aren't lawful;
Nooses give;
Gas smells awful;
You might as well live.

—DOROTHY PARKER

Two months after Clark's death, I was not eating very much. I had become quite thin. My face was drawn, and in the photographs taken of me there is a haunted, tight quality about my mouth. I had aged quickly in the weeks since Clark went into the garage in his house in St. Paul, Minnesota, and turned on the engine of his Subaru station wagon, started up the tape recorder and began to talk his death. Like talking blues. His favorite. All the blues singers, talking their blues while they described their troubles, playing the guitar behind the sad stories. Perhaps if he had lived, he might have set the words to music, like a suicide rap.

Iris Bolton, the author of *My Son . . . My Son . . . A Guide to Healing After Death, Loss, or Suicide,* held my hand through the first weeks and months after Clark's death. She had lost her son when he was nineteen, when he went into his bedroom and put a bullet through his head. She is a therapist, her life devoted to saving others. She could not save her son, and had written a deeply moving and important book about his death, and she and I were introduced shortly after Clark killed himself. She helped me survive the first few agonizing weeks and months.

But as time went on, I grew more fragile and felt as weak as I had ever felt in my life. The flame of my will to live and create, to go through the terrible dark wood in which I found myself, was burning low. It had always roared through whatever was in my path, and now I was frightened. The old will to live and to do, and think and be, was flickering.

Although I had started to do some recovery work, seeing therapists, going to other groups, meditating and talking with friends and family about my loss, and theirs, Louis thought I needed more help than I was getting in the city and made arrangements for us to go to the Canyon Ranch facility in Lenox, Massachusetts.

·   ·   ·

I met Louis Nelson in 1978, four days before I went into treatment for alcoholism. My friend Jeanne Livingston was dating Louis's then business partner, Bob Gersin, and she wanted to arrange a blind date. Having just been through a painful breakup with a man I had lived with on and off for four years, I resisted, but Jeanne's persistence won out. On meeting Louis, I was struck by his good looks, his bright blue eyes, beautiful full beard, mustache, eyebrows that grew wondrously upward. He is Norwegian, and looks it, with that glint in his eye and his solid, handsome, engaging presence. He was somehow present in a way that no man had been for me before. I felt that warmth, a tenderness and yet a solid sturdiness, and I was smitten.

It took me a few weeks to find this handsome, kind, loving man again because I went off to get sober at a treatment center in Pennsylvania and came home to New York to discover a new world in which everything would change. We had our first official date in July and have been together ever since. But the rings we exchanged at our wedding, eighteen years after we met, bear the date of April 16, 1978, when we met and both our worlds changed.

Louis is a man of great strength and talent. He is an industrial designer, a creative, imaginative man, full of elegant ideas and a deep desire to make things that are beautiful for the world's edification.

On our first real dinner date, at Orsini's in New York, we talked all night, till the waiters stood around looking at their watches and flicking their towels over their arms, and rolling their eyes. As the hours went by, we talked about everything. I had told Louis what I had done, and he had asked me, when we talked on the phone, which we did many times between our first meeting and our first date, whether I didn't think my life was going to change dramatically now that I was sober. He knew, much better than I, what a momentous change would occur now that I was not using alcohol to solve every problem that came my way.

We left the restaurant, to the waiters' relief, but reluctantly, near midnight. As we stood on Sixth Avenue, I wondered if Louis would simply put me in a cab. He got me a cab, got in with me, drove me home, and kissed me at the door. Chaste, and promising, and delicious. I quickly realized I was over the moon about this man, who was a gift of sobriety, a gift of time, and a gift from God. I always think of Louis as a gift from my Higher Power, and in the days to come after we became more intimate and realized this was for real, something neither of us had ever experienced, all I could do was pray, Let it be true, God's will be done.

Before long, we were living together. I was struggling with Clark and his problems, his schools, and becoming clear about my relationship with Clark, in a new and sober way. Louis and Clark became close over the coming years, and I know Clark loved the man who was my partner, and would become my husband. Recently Louis and I were talking about the distance we have come together, as a couple. Being married has brought us closer together, in ways I would never have dreamed. The old ceremonies, with their promises, and their depth, have helped us to grow spiritually together, as well as emotionally. We pray together, and laugh together as well. We are not embarrassed to share the deepest secrets, and the silliest jokes. It is miraculous,

I think, after all the years of chaotic relationships that studded my earlier life.

And Louis continually amazes me. We were talking about our books recently—he is writing a book about memorials, following his work on the Korean War Veterans Memorial, and I have been working on this journey of my experience with suicide. There are many similarities in what we are walking through separately, and one of the things we talk about is how often, at a funeral, you learn so much more about someone than you ever dreamed of learning, even if you have known the person for a very long time. Stories are told, pictures are painted through people's memories, and I have often come away from a funeral thinking, my, I am astonished to know these things.

Louis mused that this may be because in death, the mask of life is lifted from the departed, leaving the clear, clean spirit to be immersed in the memories and the hearts of those they have left behind. What you see is memory and spirit, revealed.

As the years went by, Louis and I would look at each other with amazement. Six years, that had been my limit in any of my previous relationships. Louis had been married twice before and didn't really think in the beginning that he was ready for another long-term commitment. I don't think I even had the capacity before meeting Louis to know what a long-term commitment was. At seven years, we were both amazed. He sold his apartment and we were living together, for real. At ten years, we were surprised and more in love than ever. At thirteen years, when Clark took his life, there were many difficult times to get through. Louis was there for me and my family in a way that was supportive and loving, and he became almost a fourth son to my mother, even more now that Ingrid, his mother, is gone. He has been a gentle, loving, caring presence, and a few years after Clark's death, we were married at St. John the Divine in New York. All our families were there, Louis's mother, Ingrid, and father, Louis; Louis's sister Dorothy, and her companion, Elaine; my mother, Marjorie; brother David and his daughter Natily; brother Michael and his son Matt; brother Denver, his wife Allison, and their children, Corrina and Josh; sister Holly, her husband Harvey, and their children Kalen, Aidan, and Rowen, our granddaughter, Hollis, Clark's child, who was the ring-bearer.

It was a glorious wedding, and Louis, now my husband, glowed, handsome in his wedding suit, and read a poem at the ceremony, a lyric and loving poem that brought tears to my eyes. Our wedding brought the years and family and the joy and love between us together in a way that we will always cherish. Together, we are more than apart, and Louis is my friend, my husband, my lover, companion and partner. I am truly blessed.

As he was finishing the Korean War Veterans Memorial, Louis started writing poems about walls—those you can see, those of steel and concrete, those that live in the mind. The Korean Memorial is a wall of faces, and the poetry he wrote was inspiring. I told him I thought I could work on a song to reflect his thoughts, and wrote a song, with lyrics by Louis and me.

Walls

We are not forgotten anymore—

Listen to my heart, look into my eyes.
I have seen the stars falling from the skies.

Listen to my fears, yours will lift and fly.
Let me show you where, I have touched the air.
Stories from the past, each as true as mine.
We can speak at last through the sands of time.
We are not forgotten anymore. . . .

These are things I know, trampled fields of snow
Sheets of falling rain, hope that conquers pain.
Souls that call again in my memory,
Through the veils of light falling on the sea.
Letters wrapped in love, lips pressed in my dreams.
Holy thoughts and brave, men who laugh and weep
We are not forgotten anymore.

I am the face on the wall,
Spirit of hope ever rising
I am the prayer in your heart for peace.

Nothing can protect us like a wall.
From our foes and our fears.
Nothing can be broken like a wall.
With our hopes and our tears.

We learned all too well, hard as you may try.
There are days you win; there are days you die.
Having seen the war, we can speak of peace.
How we prayed all night for the dawn's release.
Did we all come home; did we turn the page?
There are walls of joy, there are walls of rage.
Walls at which you weep, walls on which you dance

Walls made of regret, walls you made by chance.
Walls that break you heart, walls through which you
can see.
Walls made in your mind, walls that set you free.
We are not forgotten anymore.

I am the face on the wall,
Spirit of hope ever rising
I am the prayer in your heart for peace.

That day in March, Louis and I drove up through the snow-powdered pine trees and the long winding stretches of the New York State Thruway. There was a gray, foggy sky, and sprinkles of snow caught on the hood and the windshield of Louis's silver Jaguar as it slid past the silhouettes of the trees. Black crows, as big as I had seen, flew between the white and green snow and trees, cawing as they went. All was silent except for their calls and the sound of the tires against wet, slick tarmac. The miles rolled under our wheels, and when we turned on the radio to search for *All Things Considered*, the sound of the suddenly meaningless talk fell like heavy fog into the car, and I asked him to turn off the radio. It was too painful to listen to words that for the moment meant nothing to me.

Very little in my life seemed to have any meaning. I thought, Why me, and then thought of Seneca, who asked, Why not me? Why not you? Why are you different, why am I different from the rest of humanity? These things happen, hard things happen. The human race is at war with itself, and to be in the war, you have to feel pain.

I didn't want to listen to Seneca. "Why me?" still pounded in my ears through the silence and the flight of crows and the green pines in the gray, cloud-shrouded whiteness of a storm that wouldn't fully break, a blizzard that refused to enclose the sky, and the car, and our lives, threatening, only, to break.

We got settled in at Canyon Ranch in the Berkshires, shook our tired bodies into leisure clothes and headed down to the dining room, where we ate salads with jet-fuel dressing, lean vinegar and slightly salted oil, pungent on fresh greens. There were grilled chicken fillets, as I remember, and slowly my tongue began to thaw, and Louis and I spoke, quietly, and then more naturally.

At a table adjoining ours, a man and his wife, gray-haired and kind-looking, sat eating their portions of salad with jet-fuel dressing. One of the directors approached our table, as the fruit and clear tea were being served, and asked, "Do you know Harold and Suzette Kushner?" We were introduced to the writer and his wife, and sat together, sharing our grief. They had lost a child, too, and it was only later that I learned how much Harold really knew about suicide.

Kushner's book, *Why Bad Things Happen to Good People*, had just been published. He brought me a copy the next day, signed, and I read it eagerly, like someone starving for information. Yes, why me? Harold's book answered so many questions. Talking to Harold and Suzette, walking in the woods, swimming in the pool, getting my heart pounding on the Stair-Master, and doing Tai Chi in the afternoon sessions, began to ease the tensions in my body and in my heart. Those meals, with the jet-fuel dressing on the salad, and the fruit and tea for desert, and the talks with Harold and Suzette, made me feel more human. I may have been in pain, but others had been there. I could make it out.

The woods were full of snow, and the storm had broken and passed. The sun shone with a bright intensity that hurt the eyes. Louis and I sweated and ran, swam and roasted in the sauna. We talked and even began to laugh once in a while. My husband's prescription for renewal and rejuvenation was perfect. I had a number of sessions with a wonderful healer named Deborah Morris Coryell. (Deborah, who created many of the healing techniques at Canyon Ranch, has gone on to direct the Shiva Foundation in Santa Fe, where she helps survivors of catastrophic loss.) She took me under her wing and explained to me that what I had experienced was what was called catastrophic loss. If I could process the feelings, go straight to the heart of the matter, I could find gifts there, waiting for me. Slowly I have come to discover some of these gifts—compassion, creativity, beauty, understanding, surrender, and the knowledge that my son will never be far from me, that his sweet spirit will be guiding me wherever I go, whatever I do. We did not talk much about suicide, we talked about survival. About spiritual growth in the new conditions of my life in which I found myself. I was greatly relieved by the talks with Deborah, and found her to be a healing, powerful teacher. Louis and I left feeling more sure we would heal, survive, and go on with our lives. It was a powerful feeling that we could live through this.

I had a copy of Clark's tape and had read the transcript but had not been able to face hearing his voice. A few weeks after my return from the Berkshires, more rested, perhaps more angry, not in as much shock, I took the tape Clark made of his dying words to the chapel in St. Bartholomew's church in Manhattan, where Clark and his daughter Hollis were christened in 1988.

By candlelight, under the embracing wings of the white marble angel, I heard Clark speak to his friends, to his father, to his wife Alyson, his daughter Hollis, to his cousin Luke, to Terry.

To me.

And to the God of his understanding.

CHAPTER 7

Suicide *and* the Soul

Don't hurry, You are going to live forever —somewhere.
In fact, you are in eternity now; so why rush?

—EMMET FOX, *AROUND THE YEAR*
WITH EMMET FOX

JOURNAL ENTRY, FEBRUARY 10, 2000

I dreamed of my son three nights ago. He came to me at the age of twelve or thirteen, red-haired, sweet-faced, innocent. He was on his way to camp, all the name tags sewn onto his clothes, his bags packed, and the schedule for his trip arranged. "When will I get to see you?" I said as I kissed his freckled nose, his smooth cheeks. "Mom," he said, wrinkling his nose and smiling at me with the indulgence of a ten-year-old for his mother's overindulgence, but with sympathy, "they really don't like the parents hanging around camp." So saying, he was off, the summer like a world of wonders laid out before him, parents' week circled on my calendar.

I live on one side of the veil, he lives on the other. He is with my father, Charlie; he is with Bill and Bob and Jim Henson, my old friend, with his grandfathers and grandmother, with Laurie, the Swedish farmer he never knew, and with Milton, the poet. He is here, I am here; he is there, and I am there. We are living in a forever time; I touch that feeling in dreams, in music, in the fullness that throbs in my heart when day breaks, when the sun shines on the snow, when the candles are extinguished and the light of the spirit shines in my darkened room.

I live in eternity's light with those I love, bound by the laws of heaven, the laws of Karma, the sense and beating of the heart. Thank God for the here, and the hereafter; I am part of them both.

At the beginning, the path before me opened like a cavern, howling with the cry of a dark, ghostly presence. How was I to make the journey into that dark cave, through the mysteries and past the nightmares? How would I travel such a great distance? How was I going to see the gift in suicide, in this tragedy? Where would I go to find answers to my questions and solace for my tears? I could not even imagine the answers to those questions. But I would have to, in order to live.

Stephen Levine, in *Who Dies,* says, "Every one who dies leaves a skeleton in his closet; but the suicide leaves one in yours." I knew I couldn't ignore the skeleton, couldn't make the event of my son's suicide a secret that would bring its own torture and its own retribution. Facing my demons has meant refusing to remain silent, refusing to accept the shame of the last taboo, for today suicide *is* the last taboo. Facing suicide has meant weeping tears I didn't know I had to shed. Looking has meant testing my own faith and my own fear. Beautiful, terrible—surviving suicide has been another path from fear to faith.

How sharp the thorn, how bright the rose of memory, how piercing the pain, as though just today it had happened. Remembering is always like a cold shot of ice in my heart, like the first stab of the sword, deep, leaving its deadly wound. And how cold the winter was without him. I knew I could not go around the terrible place I now have come to know so very well. I had to go through it.

Though I had been on a journey of the spirit before my son died, and had meditated for many years, the death of my beloved son has been a powerful teacher. It is nearly ten years since he died, and in these past years, I have come to think of suicide, and suicide survival, as spiritual issues, with spiritual answers that have come from the pain and the sorrow. Suicide has seemed always to do with the soul and with faith—a lack of faith or a deep sense of faith. Leonard Cohen says, "There is a hole in everything, that's how the light gets in." Without the wound there is no miracle. And I know these wounds are the entrance to a power greater than I am—an entrance to God, and, once more, to grace. Without it I am doomed.

Albert Camus describes suicide as the one truly serious philosophical problem in life: "Judging whether life is or is not worth living amounts to answering the fundamental question of philosophy. All the rest—whether or not the world has three dimensions, whether the mind has nine or twelve categories—comes afterwards." But reading about the philosophical questions that suicide brings up seems clean and crisp. Surviving suicide doesn't feel like that. Living through it is messy and emotionally as well as physically painful. Camus, and others, sound so academic, so clinical. Living through it feels like having your heart cut open with no anesthetic.

Faith has become my teacher, and death and loss and the sound of pounding waves and the pounding of blood in my own veins, singing to me that living fully and completely is the only way to travel from this darkness to the blazing light. I watch and listen as my daughter-in-law, and my granddaughter, and my loving and wounded family, find their way through this loss. My beloved husband Louis, with whom I have traveled this path, shares in every day and in every year, as Clark's death reaches the first decade of memory. My family, who loved him so, talks about Clark, about his laughter, his humor, his intensity, and his funny quirks. I have come to see that the laughter is so healing, and talking of my son's goodness and his foibles eases the pain and makes us all realize he is with us, forever, in spirit.

Even as I put one foot in front of the other, show up for my life, and the lives of my loved ones, learning to survive, I shiver when someone's suicide is mentioned, and the chill makes its way from my lips to my heart as I speak of my own journey, as I tell another survivor the things I did, the actions I took, the way I moved from the initial terrible day of his death to this day. Putting the journey into words is one of the only ways I have found to warm the chill in my heart, to speak to another wounded healer.

Dark days followed the first, the only death. As the weeks and then the months passed, and then the years, I learned to hold the words like stones in my mouth. Suicide. Survivor. New words, old, ancient, terrible words.

When Clark died, I found there was very little written about surviving the suicide of a loved one. Four books, Stephen Levine's *Who Dies*, Iris Bolton's *My Son . . . My Son*, Christopher Lukas's *Silent Grief*, and A. Alvarez's *The Savage God*, were sent to me by friends, smuggled, as it felt, into my solitary, terrible, confinement, giving me some solace. The society that once took the horror of suicide out on its survivors, denying them spiritual and social healing resources, condemning the soul of their departed loved one to perpetual torment in hell, and hiding the terrible wound in shame, layer upon layer, had little to offer in this enlightened, progressive time.

My time—our time—had little to say to me, to all of us, for my son left his wife and daughter and a large, loving, beautiful family and friends to mourn his death. In the aftermath of his suicide, all perceptions changed, all bets were off as to how we, together and individually, would weather the storm of being suicide survivors. We knew nothing about how to do it. We only knew we had lost our most beloved son, father, husband, cousin, nephew, and friend. Ten years later, we are learning how in the world to do this, to be suicide survivors.

There were friends who helped then, and continue to help. Louis suffered so much, too, and people called, they came to see us, wrote letters, sent books. When I could sit still, read, be in my own skin, quietly, I read these books about suicide and survival. There were writers I had known before, and some I was led to by those who had already traveled the dark road from tragedy and sorrow back to life, back to more than survival. As I was stronger, and could concentrate, I read these books, drank them in as though I were drinking from the waters of an oasis of pure spring water bubbling from a well in the middle of the desert, sweet as honey, dark as blood. I found some comfort—I was not the first, and I would not be the last, who would lose a child or a loved one to suicide. I was not the last who would try to take my own life.

And there are friends who understand the blight in my life and the lives of my family. When I am with them and the talk is all about children, about sons and daughters graduating from school, about children reaching my son's age (Clark was thirty-three when he died) and becoming partners in their law firms, successes in their careers, parents of their own children, these friends will give me a look, or call me later, or take me aside, to say they understand how heavy my heart probably feels at those moments. Suicide blasts your world apart, and no matter how many years go by, there is still that yawning cave. I thank God for those who understand and try in their own ways to ease my pain and shore up my loss with the gift of their presence, and their understanding.

"Catastrophic" was what the grief was called. What had happened to all of us, and for me, his mother (it was comforting to be told, and finally believe, that I will always be his mother) was a catastrophic loss. I couldn't eat for weeks, didn't really sleep, wandering around like some lost person, not knowing if I were a danger to myself. I couldn't tell how I felt, or when I felt, what it was that I was feeling. The loss was deep and mysterious; it could have been nothing, everything, that had died. In a way, it was like the elephant that we hadn't spoken of in childhood that hovered around us, the alcoholism and the alcoholic, in my family. From one side, it felt one way, from the other, like a totally different creature. There seemed no way to put the picture together, and get an elephant, or a suicide, out of all the different views. I knew, at moments, that looking would destroy me, but couldn't turn my eyes away, for that way was destruction, too. Why is the mystery of the act so deep and so compelling? I don't mean to contemplate, in the sense of thinking of my own death, for I don't, a day at a time, go to that place. But surviving my son's action seems to demand a universe of exploration.

For those of us with depression, with reasons, with pains that feel unbearable, suicide can be alluring, compelling, and seductive. But Dr. Edwin Shneidman, a leading authority on suicide, says that, although many depressed people take their own lives, many suicides are not depressed and that suicide can be, of itself, an illness, a turn of thinking, a reasonable choice, not that of a depressed person.

At many times in history, suicide has been a solution to a variety of problems, and has often been considered an honorable, even desirable way to die; in others cultures, and other times, most recently in our own, suicide has been believed to be illegal, or immoral. Many times unforgivable.

According to research published in *Time* magazine as recently as January 20, 2003, suicide is the leading cause of death among people between the ages of fifteen and twenty-four. Suicide is at its highest level over the age of sixty-five. Other causes of death are highlighted in gray, such as stroke, cerebral palsy, etc. Suicide is highlighted in black.

Suicide is a major cause of death among teenagers. These are messages of pain and fear, hopelessness and despair that drive these disparate, and desperate, individuals to try to take their own lives. It is said that most of these attempts are cries for help, and that no attempt is halfhearted, that all are serious and should be taken as such. And all suicide attempts have at least some chance of leading to death.

Every year, 31,000 people in the United States, 15,000 of them teenagers, succeed in their suicide attempts, and for each person who succeeds, it is said that an average of ten people must suffer the pain of being suicide survivors. That is the rub, and that is where the solution may be found; the light must shine not just on one kind of suicidal preoccupation or danger to the self, but on all, leaving no stone unturned in the search for answers.

After the death of my son, a woman whose father had been a Catholic shared with me that when her father had taken his own life, the priest told her mother that her husband could be buried in the cemetery, but he could not be borne in the hearse through the entrance in the customary manner; instead, he would have to be carried in his casket over the closed gates.

The image and the pain of that family seared my heart. How heartless, how primitive, how devastating to his family and friends. Not to be able to celebrate the transformation of a loved one's life, not to see his death as an illness instead of a sin—not to ease his spirit to the hereafter! Jesus wept, as they say.

Another survivor of a parent's suicide, when she was seven or eight, admitted that when her father had died, his name was simply never mentioned again in her family, until the time she herself was in her forties. Even his tombstone did not bear his name. When she was an adult, in her forties, she began the painful work of remembering, naming, and mourning her long-dead father.

For centuries, suicides have had to deal with the condemnation of the church and state. The church has in recent years softened its stance on suicide. Still suicide is a taboo in discussion and treatment, and the issue of suicide is pushed aside, dealt with only rarely.

A. Alvarez tells us in his book, *The Savage God,* of the suicides of Christian martyrs, of whom John Donne wrote: "Many were baptized only because they would be burnt." Out of the fire and into heaven, in other words. There are all kinds of suicides, from the euthanasia that some have sought in the last painful stages of a terminal disease to the streets of Saigon when Buddhist monks burned themselves alive because of their political beliefs. Throughout time, people have chosen to end their lives: Petronius; Hero, who drowned in the Hellespont; Seneca and Socrates, out of favor in their times; Cleopatra, the asp biting her and memorializing her; the Jews at Masada who chose mass suicide rather than face enslavement by the Romans; the Japanese who chose *seppuku* over surrender; Jocasta and Portia; Marilyn Monroe; Hart Crane; Cesare Pavese; Virginia Woolf; Hemingway, his father, and his granddaughter, Margaux; a daughter of Karl Marx; sons of Eugene O'Neill, Robert Frost, and Herman Melville; the daughter of George McGovern; the son of Carroll O'Connor. My son.

Some were the product of societies where it was honorable and respectable to commit suicide. Some were the result of the use of drugs and alcohol, combined with depression and mental illness. Kurt Cobain shot himself while high on heroin.

Geo Stone says:

> *Excess alcohol and other drug use are often associated with suicide. The observed high correspondence between alcohol and suicide can be explained in several ways, including: (a) Alcoholism can cause loss of friends, family, and job, leading to social isolation. (This may be a chicken-and-egg question; it's equally plausible that family or job problems induce the excess alcohol use. In its later stages, the fact and consequences of alcoholism dominate the picture and are often blamed for everything.); (b) Alcohol and suicide may both be attempts to deal with depression and misery; (c) Alcohol will increase the effects of other sedative drugs, frequently used in suicide attempts; (d) Alcohol may increase impulsive actions.*

Suicide has been with us in every age, in every country, in every kind of family, rich, poor, scholar, poet. Children, some of them under ten years of age.

It is difficult to explain to a young person what suicide is—and what it means. In an incident I heard of recently, when parents learned that their teenagers were being given a course about suicide in high school, they refused to allow the teacher, who understood the terrible, unusually high suicide rate among teenagers, to continue the course.

The vision of Clark's suicide has left a second image planted on my heart, like a double exposure, a picture of my own life and its impact on my son's death. The vision reverberates with what I think I might have done wrong, what I might have said or not said that might have caused the black figure that haunts my memories to have come to such children of light as we were; for all my meditations did not keep death and tragedy away.

How was it that I *felt* to blame? I am the mother. I am the adult. I am the older one, the one who knew about this place he ventured, having been there myself, having tried. I never talked much about my attempt with him, never truly shared my own journey to the edge of the night. Had I said as much as I might? My own attempt was long ago, when I was much younger than he was at his death. And I had explained my own attempt away in year after year of therapy. I wasn't drinking, I was fourteen, and yet, I had tried to take my life. Perhaps it was not a very serious attempt, for after all, I lived. But by now, I know all our attempts are serious.

And in spite of the comforting voice of my son in my meditations, I was living by a thread, feeling sorrow, and despair. And, contrary to what I knew was logical, I felt guilt.

But a few days after Clark's death, Joan Rivers called me to connect, to share with another survivor. Her husband had taken his own life, and she had been contacted by mutual friends about Clark's death. There is a network of wonderful people who did this, holding out their hands and their hearts to me, to help me to step from horror to the world of the living again. Joan was comforting and generous, and has been a fellow sufferer and a fellow witness to the gift that comes from talking about suicide publicly, helping others to heal from the wound, both in her television movie about suicide, and her personal talks with me, sometimes in person, sometimes from the dressing rooms of her backstage shows in cities around the country.

Her voice at the other end of a telephone line often got me through another night.

The first thing I was told by my wise friends, who had lost children, husbands, friends, parents of their own, was that there are no guilts in suicide. I believed them, even though I felt too weak to walk or think straight. I wept, knowing they were right, must be right. I had tried to do everything I could to help my son, but Clark was an adult. He was thirty-three. He was a man, a father, and a husband. I couldn't fight Clark's demons, and he fought them and lost. Or won, depending on your definition of faith.

There have been gifts I could not recognize at first. I have experienced the rebirth of joy, the feeling that I am living in the sunlight of the spirit, that God's hand is always in mine, and that He will not take me to a place where I cannot find meaning, in which I cannot be of service.

As my own guilt began to subside and I heard the voices of others who had walked the path that I was on, I began to realize that my son's suicide was a choice I had to honor, rather than take as an attempt on my own life, an unacceptable act that tore my heart apart. I began to see that this is just another path to acceptance, and surrender. When I began to accept this terrible action as my son's path and his destiny, I began to forgive him and myself and to find a way out of the dark place.

CHAPTER 8

The Path

About suffering they were never wrong,
The old masters: how well they understood
Its human position; how it takes place
While someone else is eating or opening a window or just
walking dully along.

—W. H. AUDEN

JOURNAL ENTRY, OCTOBER 7, 1994

Your hearing changes, you detect subtle shifts in the wind. In the pit of the stomach, I know things I didn't know before. I don't have to think about what is important, I feel it in the gut and there is nothing I can do to think my way out of loneliness, of despair, I must feel these things—they fly into the window on a sunny day and settle on the eggs and the waffles, they pour over my heart while I am watching a deer run across the road in the lights of the car on a summer night; they find their way into my dreams, where the silence from that particular corner of my mind where you live forever rings, like a bell that tolls with no sound, and sometimes I must remind myself that the bell is for you, my beloved, my present and my unpresent flesh and blood, my heir to grief and sorrow, my inheritor of light, my redheaded once and forever and only one, Clark, my son.

I look into a book in which I have written, before or after your death, I don't know which; Gratitude—for clarity, music, poetry, Louis, Hollis, my family, my friends, my eyes, my ears, my body that works so well, my sponsor, my lessons, my animals, my home, my bed, coffee in the morning, prayer at night, walking prayer, my imagination, oatmeal cookies, hour meetings, the birds singing, the moon shining, the sun, blue eyes, the President, *Amazing Grace*, Clark who is my greatest teacher next to God.

You are with me forever, in me forever, part of me forever.

> *There are no stars tonight but those of memory.*
> —HART CRANE

I live in Manhattan. I know my way pretty well around this city, its parks and its rivers, its shadowed corridors. In the noisy borough of Manhattan between the tides of Spuyten Duyvil in the East River and the broad reaches of the Hudson as it runs by my windows on the West Side, glimmering in the sunset and the dawn, I have found a home and a reason, friends and dreams, sorrow and hope. I know the churches where, in leaded glass windows, I have seen the faces of the angels, and lit candles in the soft light to the saints and to God. I know the skyscrapers in Manhattan's middle and in its water-garlanded downtown reaches, and the brownstones along the side streets of flowering trees in Chelsea and Greenwich Village. I have walked in snowstorms on these streets, hunted the addresses of friends and therapists, dentists and doctors, lawyers and practitioners of the heart and the body and the soul.

I somehow still don't expect sorrow or tragedy to live here. I keep an optimistic eye on the weather, on my inner storms, even.

But I know another place that is on no map, that can be found in every city there ever was, on every riverbank, on each and every street that was ever walked and lived upon. I know the location, and the tragedy, of suicide. At home, I would hear the voices call as I looked down from my windows on the trees where the warble of purple finches on their way south sang to me; they would call to me in the call of the train that still runs along the river and whistles through my quiet and turbulent nights, from the depth of the shadows by the water; I would not have expected to find this place of secrets and dark shadows, a place of dark figures that stands on either side of an opening into the universe, or to heaven, or to hell, whose only true address is tears.

In the pain and anguish that followed Clark's death, and the slow understanding that this loss would never go away, would always be a part of my life, always there, not going to vanish, no matter how much therapy I might have, no matter how many times I might feel I "understood" my loss, I realized I needed to be talking to people who had experienced similar loss. Louis and I became regulars at a suicide survivors group at Regency Hospital, on the East Side of Manhattan.

Spring was moving in the air by then, January's cold and snow melting, receding as I counted the days since Clark's death, and in the city, the flowers along Park Avenue were blossoming, pink cherry and white daffodils in plots, violet iris waving in the wind of the traffic roaring past, going anywhere fast. How could they bloom, I would think, when he is dead?

I already knew that dark place where the earth opened like the mouth to a cave among ordinary streets, where all was light and relief, where all was peace and surrender, where every problem was solved. I knew the lure, the seduction, of those beckoning figures around the doors of the grave.

There were times when the soft whisper of the calling voices around the edge of this place beckoned to me—this would solve everything, this would be the simplest way, this would mean that I wouldn't have to suffer any more. This would mean that the darkness around my heart would vanish. Ah, the voices would say, they would miss you, but they do not love you anyway, at least not enough to make up for this terrible voice that calls to you from that dark place. Come here, the voices call, come to where we can put you to sleep, forever.

I knew those voices. And I knew it would be easier to attempt suicide than to survive it, having done both.

At the recovery group at the Regency Hospital, in the company of strangers who were to become friends, some of that vast hole began to heal. And sometimes, over those weeks and months of recovery, I thought I might make it out alive.

That first night, I met Ethel, who was sure her son had been murdered, and George, who was suing the city for negligence in his son's death from a "fall" from a bridge. Those of us who had passed the denial stage, Ann and Percy, and Daisy, a single mother, who had lost her son when he was out on a day pass from Gracie Square hospital, and a half dozen others who had lost children, brothers, sisters tried gently to ease Ethel and George into some acceptance, although the fact that they were at this formally scheduled suicide survivors meeting, having been sent by some doctor or healer of their acquaintance, gave the lie to their suspicions and accusations of the fault of the city, the murderous acts of others. There were no mistakes. Each of us had survived the death of a loved one. Each of us had a chance to share as we went around in a circle, talking of the pain, talking of the wound. I had already discovered how important it was to talk about this loss with others who had experienced similar tragedies. But this group was a gathering of people who had lost someone to suicide, and suicide is different than murder, than disaster, different than the loss of a loved one to cancer or to other illness. There are so many deep wounds that can paralyze the heart and even stop your feet from moving toward the help that might be there.

On the first night Louis and I went to Regency, we were taken by our friends Amy and Sinclair Morris, who had lost a child to suicide, and who had gone out of their way since learning of our loss to guide us, send us books, talk to us on the phone. Amy Sinclair assured us the group was safe, and a haven. Still, I was nervous, eager to tell my experience, but hesitant. Would others understand, even those who had suffered losses of their own? How could I talk about the rage I felt, the fear, the place where the universe had broken, never to be mended? Would other people think I was crazy? I felt unusually timid.

The therapist in this group was a young, willowy woman named Maude, whom I mistakenly judged to be incompetent and inappropriate at first, out of her depth with this grief, because she was not herself a survivor. I resented the fact that she had no personal experience of suicide survival. How wrong I was, for in the few weeks Louis and I went to the Regency group, as she heard our stories, Maude discovered what she recognized as a suicide in her close family, a nephew who had killed himself in a car. She began the mourning of this young man, a mourning uncompleted at his death, because the mourning of a suicide involves more information, and more pain, than the mourning of a "normal," even a sudden and violent, death. After that, I saw Maude as competent, and appropriate. She had done a lot of work herself, and as a result, she was "accepted" into the main purpose. "Like heals like," the homeopaths say. What comes from the heart reaches the heart. Maude's heart had been opened, and her professionalism enhanced, from her discovery of the link between our lives, our losses, and hers.

In the conference room of Regency, in the calm, still center of New York, a siren would occasionally break the stillness. The faces of our group were still and, for the moment, healed.

Between the meetings at Regency, I started to write prayers to get me through these days, something I had done at other times in my life, but now I was in the trenches, and had to write them, not as therapy, but as survival tools. So I sat in silence above the river there in my home, writing. I had gotten phone numbers of some of the people in the group, and got to know a couple of them better.

That first night it was a small group, and I was struck by the fact that many of the survivors were on medication for their grief. I wanted to feel everything, the pain and the depression, the hurt, even the rage. Iris had told me that people don't heal as easily if they use drugs to get through the grief, and as she had twenty years of experience as a therapist, was herself a survivor, and had the heart of an angel and the steely determination of a realist, I believed her. I did not know if I could survive it, but I knew I wanted to feel it all, and find a way to face it now so that it would not haunt me in years to come, rising suddenly from the mists of secrecy.

The Regency survivors group gave me hope. Sometimes, at first, I felt I was an outsider even as I needed to hear survivors speak of how they were making their way through these terrible seas. It was one of those mysterious gifts we who live in New York and other cities find among the grit and the drama of our urban existences.

Still, it was a surprisingly healing and wonderful place to land. And land I did.

Maude's discovery of her nephew's suicide was something that she only spoke of in swift, short paragraphs. Now, all of us in the group knew she was one of us, though none of us asked, specifically, for details. I suppose we knew that when she was ready, she would tell us what it was that had made her so understanding, such a voice of compassion, among us, the survivors. Maude would tell, eventually, of her own experience. We waited, patiently, knowing the story would unfold sometime in the future, and living, as we had to do, one day, one meeting, one conversation on the telephone, at a time.

On this particular night, Maude announced that we were to have a guest and called for a girl of about twenty to join us. The group shifted, swimming like a school of fish, and opened enough to allow in the young woman—an attractive brunette of medium height, with big brown eyes who was dressed in a white shirt, cotton pants, and a tan jacket. She would have to prove her membership in the group, and there was a space around her, the new fish, the new face, the new mystery.

"Carol has been in the hospital here, recovering from her last suicide attempt," Maude told us. There was an audible gasp, as each of us judged our alignment with her, enemy or friend. Carol began to talk, eager to tell us her story. In that story of her cares, her "reasons," her fight with depression, with alcohol, with drugs, Carol became the child we had lost, the son, the daughter, the parent, sibling. We were the ones who were left, and each had our share of anger, and rage, and compassion, for the other.

"But someone can help you, Carol," George kept saying. "Can't you go to AA? Or take Prozac?" Carol had been in AA, and been on Prozac, and a litany of other drugs none of us could pronounce. She had tried many times in her life to get off the planet, and always came to. She told us she had no control over her attempts. She wondered if anyone in her family would care, and we assured her that they would, that we cared, that she had a choice. She explained her reasons, and we explained our sorrow.

I don't know if Carol ever tried again to take her own life. I would imagine she probably did, and that our evening with her did not dissuade her, but we were the Greek chorus of her contemplated death, giving her a glimpse of the devastation that could be left behind in the wake of her suicide. We sat as though in a daze after we had heard Carol speak. As her voice drifted into the silence remaining in the room, I thought about the power in the intimacy that comes with sharing secrets, and how talking about all of this was healing me, and, I believe, the others who were there with me. The experience emphasized again what I believe is a great source of healing that exists in breaking the secrets. When they are broken, no matter how imperfectly, answers will come. What I know of suicide—the mystery, the tragedy, I can speak of, and of the hope that brought me from dark waters to the light of a new day; for there is hope. I will always need to put into words the inexplicable feelings of the deep waters where all of us who are survivors swim, live, and breathe every day. I, like those who have gone to that strange inner sea and come back, only can tell how we sailed, how we swam those seas, and how, even through tragedy, we can be reborn.

"I feel so strongly that what all of you have been talking about is a spiritual journey," Maude said at the next Wednesday night meeting, after we had made ourselves comfortable in the circle, widening tonight to let in two newcomers. "I mean, in order to survive this, you all are having to dig into your souls and find out who you really are, am I right?" There was silence in the room, except for the muffled sound of tears from a newcomer, a disheveled, pretty woman in her forties whose name was Malinda and who had come to the meeting with her mother, Sally, who sat as though frozen, carved in stone, silent, her mouth in a thin line. My eyes went around the room, wondering who would respond to Maude's question, Ethel, Louis, Sam, perhaps. Maybe George, who looked less angry tonight and whose hands had stopped shaking. Percy, perhaps. Daisy, I thought, who had talked to me a great deal on the telephone about her dark journey of the spirit since her son's suicide.

"I know who I am," said Sally, Malinda's mother, the newcomer, surprising us entirely. "I go to church, I read the Bible, I support my daughter's choices, and her loss feels like my loss. But there is nothing about me that has to be changed. I know who I am." She shuffled stiffly in her chair, avoiding the wet-eyed, dagger-like look from her daughter. "What I want to know is, who did he think *he* was? Doing this to himself, destroying my daughter's life?" She looked sideways now at the young woman, who had stopped crying and was looking at her mother with what might have been loathing but was probably love. Love-hate, certainly.

"My life is not destroyed!" said her daughter.

My mind wandered from the room with my own answers to the question, as I looked over who I was now, and thought about who I was becoming.

In the first place, I knew this had to be a spiritual journey. Everything is, after all, and in the end we all lose everything. One life equals one death, one way or the other. The odds are very good of that. But how the death, how the life? I could feel myself changed by all that had happened since the moment of my son's death.

Carla hesitated a while before starting to speak, stretching her legs, cracking the knuckles of her hands and rubbing her eyes. Maude kept very still, the room was silent. We were waiting for Carla to talk about what she had been keeping a secret for her adult life, since she was fifteen. Now in her late fifties, she had come to see Maude and our Regency suicide survivor group because, although her sister had taken her own life more than forty years earlier, Carla had begun to have anxiety attacks and to drink heavily again after many years of sobriety.

"We were fifteen, I mean I was fifteen. I mean, Leona was fifteen. We both were fifteen, although I am a few minutes older."

This brief statement had exhausted Carla and she looked around the room as though hunting for the cue cards. We all smiled gently, urging her to continue.

The sister she had lost was her twin. The family was Catholic, and suicide was looked at as something terrible and unforgivable. The body of Carla's sister was dropped into unholy ground outside the graveyard. Her simple name was written on the stone, but her name was never mentioned again in the family. Her photos were heaped on a fire and burned. Her clothes were given to the Salvation Army, all of them, even the lovely ones that a cousin, or a friend, might have liked to wear.

At the next meeting at Regency, a week later, those of us who had been attending seemed to have recovered a little, I thought. There were no new faces that night, and I felt that there was some cohesion of the group, as though carrying around each other's stories of pain for a week had relieved some of our own.

Ethel, with her white, white hair, thin and athletic looking, who had thought her son had been murdered, sat down in a straightbacked chair and leaned against her husband Sam, an attractive man, who had lost slightly the look of a lean hungry animal out to kill that he had worn for the past weeks. A softness had begun to settle on his features. He nodded to me and smiled, a brief, dazzling smile. I hadn't seen his smile before.

George, silent at the past few meetings, greeted Louis with a warmth that had not been present in our last weeks. He told us his suit against the city had been quietly dropped when the coroner had ruled out homicide and found a large quantity of drugs in his son's body, along with a note that stated the boy's intentions to end his own life.

"I still should sue the city," he said. "How is it possible that a young person could be able to buy such things on the street, anyway? Don't they know how to stop the sale of drugs?" To which the group shook a silent nod in response.

Louis and I had felt a little less devastated during the preceding week. We had gone out to dinner a couple of times with other friends, and I had gained a couple of pounds and didn't look so gaunt. Louis had dressed, as usual, with wonderful style, but his eyes were alive tonight instead of inwardly pained, and he seemed almost his old self.

Maude was quiet, commenting only briefly as she led us through our comments and memories.

"Has anyone had any breakthroughs about their feelings?" she asked, after we had settled down with Styrofoam cups of awful coffee from the big silver urn in the adjoining room. There wasn't always coffee, so we thought the gesture on the part of the hospital one of welcome, bad coffee or not.

Ann spoke up first. "I am in a rage," she said. "And I guess, for me, that is a breakthrough. Until now, I haven't been able to feel anything but total despair." Most of us nodded, feeling the rage in our own stories, our own losses.

"There is a stage of recovery from suicide that includes rage," Maude said. "It's hard to understand—since most of us spend all of our lives trying to keep alive—when someone we love doesn't feel that way about life, when they try to kill the thing we fight so hard for." Then a young man named Carl told of how his father had taken his life many years before, and the family buried his father's memory and his name, neither of which ever was spoken of again, except in this room, dozens of years later. His father had had no memorial, no memory, no words, and no talk of his goodness or his other qualities. Just a stunned silence that spanned the decades and still provoked shame and horror in this young man's voice, which shook even as he spoke.

At another meeting, Maude seemed ready to talk about her own loss.

"How did your nephew die?" I asked, finally comfortable enough with Maude to broach the question. She bent her head forward and was very quiet. I didn't think she was going to answer me, and the time had come for the meeting to start, so we moved into our seats in the circle, and began with a prayer, with which we usually started the meeting.

"God, grant me the serenity to accept the things I cannot change, courage to change the things I can, and the wisdom to know the difference."

"Thanks for coming here to help each other," Maude said. She read some announcements about upcoming meetings at the hospital, and a change of rooms, in response to which there was a sigh of resignation—we all liked our cozy, comfortable room with the red cushioned chairs and the big window that let in the sound of wind and rain, and the light of the street lamp outside the building. After we had settled down again, Maude went on.

"I think," she began, "that I have to tell you about the suicide of my nephew, or what I have come to understand was a suicide. It was a long time ago, and the feelings are still surfacing. But all of you have helped me to go through the grief and the loss of that gentle, loving boy who found a way to end his life."

He had been a delicate child, she told us, and her sister's youngest. He loved to paint and draw, but in school had a hard time with numbers, and later, with people. He had not been able, somehow, to fit in as he grew, going to high school, then college. He was put on drugs for his antisocial behavior, his depression, his bipolar condition, which was diagnosed when he was in his late twenties.

"My sister decided that she had to take another action to help him. She gave him a lot of money, the money she told him he would inherit when she and her husband died. He went out a bought a car, a bright green thing that seemed to have wings and a fancy name I can't remember. Ted seemed happy. He drove his car fast, he liked to go out into the country, get a little drunk, and race around the country roads near the town where they lived."

Ted drove the car into a tree one night. He had a girl in the car with him, who lived, though she was badly injured.

"I always thought it was just an accident," Maude said. "Then a few days after my first meeting here at Regency with all of you, I got a call from the girlfriend. She was coming to New York, she said, and wanted to see me."

In their meeting, the girlfriend, whose name was Carolyn, met with Maude, not only as a friend but also as a professional mental health care provider. At the time of Ted's death, she had been too upset to talk about the facts to anyone in her hometown, especially Ted's mother.

"She told me they went out for a few drinks, and as they did every weekend, went for a spin in the fine green car. That night, Carolyn said she didn't want Ted to drive so fast.

"'He looked at me kind of funny, got this really weird look in his eyes, and said, "I'll never drive fast again, I promise you."' He put his foot on the gas pedal, pushed it to the floor, and they flew down the road and straight into that tree." She took a breath. "So you see, he did kill himself, and he was so out of his mind that he didn't care if he took somebody else with him."

"Everybody takes people with them, even though they don't drive them into a tree," George said. He had gained some weight, and looked better than he had when I first met him at Regency. Tonight he was wearing a bright red corduroy shirt, black leather trousers, white socks, and new loafers. His glasses were smudged, and he took them off to wipe them with a white square of cotton that he pulled out of the pocket of the black pants. "There are so many victims. She is lucky she lived through the accident. But she is still a victim, like all of us."

One night at the group, it was my turn to tell about the death of my son. I was shaking as I spoke, for the feelings were as deep and as painful as they had been from the beginning of the loss of my beloved son. George was there that night, I remember, and Maude, of course, and Amy and Sinclair. Louis held my hand tightly. The room was very quiet, as though everyone were holding their breath. Outside, the sound of traffic died down to an occasional honk, the singing of a siren, like a bird's call, as I told the group about Clark, what he looked like, what his life had been like. I said my son had left victims, those who mourn his death and always will. It is just as though he took us with him in some way. I said I had had a dream about my son the night before, in which he was powerfully present in the room. When I awoke, I found myself sitting up in bed, wondering about dreams and death. Do those who die wait for dreams of us, as we wait for dreams of them?

"I'd like to read a poem I wrote about my son's death," I said. It's called "Permanent Solution." I managed to bring out a wrinkled white piece of paper and smooth it on my lap and put on my reading glasses and read, stolidly, to keep from crying:

Can't sleep tonight.
I think of you all ruined
In your final sleep,
The edge of your world tilting,
Leaving us here to swirl in confusion and questions.
How beautiful your were, there at the edge,
At the end of my world. Your skin glowed,
Almost still warm.
You were home, and I had so far to go.
Have so far to go.
Yesterday I met a woman who knew you.
She had learned you were dead, and was sad, she said.

As I am, as are all of us here in our tilted, ruined world.
I threatened, but
God damn it, you did it. How cruel and unusual
And how predictable.
Tilt. Ruin. The edge of the end.

CHAPTER 9

Suicide Bomber

*You shall love your crooked neighbor
With your crooked heart.*

—W. H. AUDEN

*Life must go on.
I forget just why.*

—EDNA ST. VINCENT MILLAY

JOURNAL ENTRY, FEBRUARY 2002
GROUND ZERO 2/11/02

It is nearly ten years since my son's death. When the World Trade Center towers went down on 9/11, it was like a rekindling of the worst of all my experiences, mostly the death of my son. They call that post-traumatic stress disorder, and I have it. We all have it, and most of us have not lost our children to suicide.

Since the tragedy of 9/11, I have come downtown several times to be near the site of our loss, to mourn, to pray, to walk the streets and look at the candles and the photographs, and to be a witness to the slow inhalation of the breath of life once again to this site of death and of destruction. Today was the first time I have been so close to this living mausoleum, the testament of absence, close to the towers that shimmer in the mind, still, that reach for the sky in the place where the sky and all our innocence came down to meet the earth.

Men and women worked today in the cold crisp air. The fires are mostly out, but smoke drifts from an occasional spot. The bathtub, built thirty years ago to hold back the Hudson River from this place, still holds. Lieutenant Jay Fagan, the young, handsome Irish father of three, who is taking my husband, some friends, and me on this tour, is a man who stood mere feet away when the first tower fell. He ran, he tells us, toward the river, dust and smoke in his face, unable to see, barely able to breathe. He is a kind man. A hero, like the rest of those who lived, and who died, in the precincts of New York. He lived through all of this, serving, and giving, comforting and soothing and weeping since the planes hit our beautiful towers and changed all of our lives. The rubble has mostly been taken away to Fresh Kill, where forensic pathologists sift every piece of evidence, still looking for DNA, for clues, for pieces to the puzzle. Men and machines are digging still, moving over the ground—hallowed, harrowed, heroed ground. They brought up five more bodies just a few days ago—all Police, four men and a woman, a captain. She and one of the men were embracing each other in death. They had lived, waiting to be found, down there where the earth was standing still under the graves of 2,800 men and women unlucky enough to have not escaped the disaster. They had lived, waiting to be found, until they died of starvation and, Lieutenant Fagan told us, dehydration.

9/11. Who would think a date, a simple combination of four strokes of the computer, the typewriter keys, four slashes of the pen, could mean such change in our lives, could alter us so very deeply. Horror and heartbreak, disbelief and rage, anger and tears; I felt them all, and over all the deep knowledge, instantly, that my life, and the lives of my family and friends, those I know and those I'll never know, will never be the same.

Suicide. They were committing suicide and took their own lives, and many of our dreams and part of each of our lives, as well. They must hate themselves for could they love themselves to do what they did? For Glory, for the lure of ten thousand or however many virgins? How is this a different kind of suicide?

At the memorial at Ground Zero the pictures and the wreaths of flowers are wilted now, even the one that says, "With love from the people of Afghanistan to the people of New York, in sympathy," are full of sorrow and remembrance.

We are grateful for the sun today. We are grateful the snow has held off so far this year, so that the work at Ground Zero can go on, unhindered by the thunderous blizzards that sometimes pound New York in the winter, piling mountains of snow and freezing streets and fingers. It has been a mild winter, as though the Gods were sending a kiss of warmth to our chilled hearts, sending us a heavenly letter of condolence.

Suicide bomber. Just the words. Suicide bomber. The words send a chill through my heart, as they are meant to do. The words mean that someone is willing to take their own life to further some political agenda, or forward some revenge upon a country, a town, a political position—an enemy.

Mesmerizing, terrifying, incomprehensible. I am a New Yorker. I wept with my city, with the world. I heard the word "suicide" over and over and it plunged its bitter sword into my heart again and again, as it is meant to do. I mean *I* am powerless to prevent, to stop it.

When the planes swept into the World Trade towers, and the devastation swept into our lives, the feeling of having lived too long and seen too much invaded our hearts. For me, and for anyone who has suffered the loss of a loved one in the past, the pain was a reliving of the horrors after my son's death—the questions, the anger, the shame, the guilt, the tumult. In addition to all the other feelings, the feeling that the world had once again come to an end could not be avoided, and that I must have brought this on myself and on my city and my world haunted my nights and thrust into my mind and heart each day.

Through the smoke and the bravery, the heroics of our firefighters and the passengers on the plane that went down in Pennsylvania, the stoic clarity of the survivors and civic leaders

and rescue workers, the faithfulness of the voices on the tele-
phones, leaving final messages or talking to their loved ones,
assuring them that they had loved and had been loved, all were
covered with the mystery and the insanity of that word—
suicide.

After 9/11, it was said that there were more pregnancies
than usual. Smoking increased by 50 percent, and alcoholism,
even in people who were sober for many years, increased. There
were AA meetings at Ground Zero that helped many of the
rescue workers deal with their frustrations and the devastating
psychological effects of pulling the bodies and body parts of
friends and strangers out of that terrible rubble. And at St.
Paul's Church on Broadway, where we saw so many messages
from people all over the world—photos and shirts and notes and
flowers—a group of volunteer counselors and physical therapists gave massages, pedicures, and TLC to hundreds of firemen
who came to the church for four-star meals prepared by the chef
David Boulez and his volunteer servers, as well as many other
people who volunteered their services to help with food and
every other kind of support.

There was more than enough service to go around in the aftermath of 9/11. People reached out from all over the world,
and the need of New Yorkers to do something in the aftermath
of the tragedy showed, in an extraordinary manner, how reaching out to help someone else can ease our own sorrow, depression, and grief.

I have begun to come out of shock, I realize. I am no longer
walking in the waking dream that pulsed through the country,
that pulsed through the city. I am taking in the change, learning

to look around at the world, at the country, with different eyes. Stunned eyes that are grateful. Three thousand people died here. Twenty thousand, they say, made it out. Three hundred forty-three of our firemen were martyred, tens of others in the recovery and police services of the city. There were people of eighty-two nationalities and countries, colors and races, who died in the towers. Those who did this thing hate what we have here, this passion for living together, for tolerating each other's differences, for celebrating them, often enough, for loving and searching and seeking and holding the pulse of America's dream—this world's dream, the miracle that is worth dying for. It is also, more than ever, worth living for.

Why would people train themselves to die, unite to destroy themselves one by one, murdering as they go, unless they are suffering from more than just political zeal? Why would they throw themselves into crowds in restaurants in Israel, fighting with the only weapons of destruction they possess, in order to create chaos and death, if not because taking their own lives is the only way they can find to express frustration, desire, anger, fury, hatred, political power, and revenge?

There is a tremendous difference between my son's taking his own life—out of frustration and fear, cornered in a situation over which he *felt* he had no control—and the girl who blew herself up only last week in a marketplace in Janin, Palestine. Still, any taking of one's life is done out of a feeling that there are no other answers. It pours out of a conviction that conflict resolution will not work (therapy, money from father, from mother, from someone to pay those overwhelming bills, someone to solve those overwhelming problems—a job, dignity, and a state, in the case of the Palestinians). No solution. No other way out. No living past midnight. Create chaos, leave the planet, one might think; it is awful anyway, and my death will be a statement. A statement of fury, or revenge, of hopelessness. Of spiritual clarity.

When the monks burned themselves alive in Saigon during the war in Vietnam, they brought attention to the situation of that terrible war and its inequities. I admired them. When a Quaker man burned himself alive on the grounds of the Pentagon during the Johnson administration, he was doing something of which I approved, not that I was not sorry he had died, but I got it—he was making a sacrifice of something that I assumed he held to be precious, his life, even the lives of his children whom he left fatherless, in the cause of something greater, more precious. Much as I mourned the necessity for his taking his own life, I understood that. Now, I searched for reasons how he was different from the girl who slit her wrists last month in Akron, a girl who was on medication, who was depressed, whose life had not gone well, who had problems with her mental stability, and a penchant for drama as well as for credit card debt. Was the monk in Saigon different from the priest who hung himself because he was guilty of molesting young men in his parish?

There are conscious as well as unconscious reasons for suicide. We would all understand the woman with cancer and her need to get out of her pain. We can understand the monk in Saigon, the Quaker, and the woman with cancer, dying painfully, in minutes and hours of incomprehensible agony, knowing there was no reason, with modern medication, for her to live in such pain. I have often heard that one of the problems in euthanasia is that doctors will not give the kind of pain medication needed to get people comfortably out of their transition from life to death. No matter what our politics, we understand that sometimes an act is symbolic, meant to attract attention to an ungodly, unholy situation. Do we feel the same about suicide terrorists? I don't know about you, but I don't. Suicides who take their own lives are one thing. Suicides who take the lives of others are another.

But was this their only way to wage the war? What about the war to change the status from within? Why not find ways to build schools, to fight the enemy by becoming what we really want to become? Is it easier to blow up children in a playground, to blow oneself up in a nightclub, taking others along? The suicide bombers who shattered the illusion of the peaceful, impenetrable freedom and ease of the United States were, I believe, ill. It would have been harder to stay home and take action against a repressive, autocratic dictatorship, harder to work toward women's rights, harder to admit the problems, and the solutions, were in front of our noses than to make a really big, terrifying statement and murder three thousand people in the process, as well as destroy any trust that might have been building in some quarters around the world that money from oil might be made to pay for schools and financial institutions, for education and a myriad of other opportunities.

The Japanese suicide kamikaze bombers in the Second World War had their purpose; it was their way to wage war. It was noble. They were given state funerals; their government honored them.

Political suicide for a "cause" does not convince me it is

"different." The rationale can be used that the poor, who have no power, must use the only weapon available. And the suicides in the name of a "good cause," say political revenge, or state security, or showing the enemy that we are not powerless, may be condoned by proud parents—as in a warrior's mother saying she is proud of her boy, that his blood was spilled for a great cause, for her cause, for the world, for freedom.

But suicide is suicide, and blood spilled in the name of political and religious, national and fanatical power is still blood spilled in a suicide and the same message is clear—there were no alternatives, we could not find the conflict resolution in our experience that would take this solution from us.

We could not find our way to plan B.

The suicide bombers have left fear, guilt, horror, terror, sorrow in their wake. They have advanced the wave of war that they adhere to—"We hate you because . . ."—fill in the blanks.

How is that different from other suicides? "They didn't love me enough, didn't give me enough, didn't do enough for me, didn't solve my problems, didn't know how to treat me. Treated me badly, couldn't heal me, couldn't read my mind, couldn't talk to me."

On that afternoon in Denver, Colorado, forty-nine years ago, when I tried and failed to kill myself, I was most definitely mentally unstable, unable to see clearly, unbalanced. I had the condition of "perfectionism"—when things must be a certain way for me to be happy, to feel loved, and if they are not this way, I am going to take my life, get out of plan A, because it is not working and I cannot see how to make it work. Suicide is often a bargaining chip in human relations, perhaps the only chip some feel they have. It is sometimes a result of mental illness and sometimes used with the intent to destroy, even up the score, punish, perhaps persuade.

Emperor Hirohito's message to the Japanese after their surrender to the United States is arguably the most effective suicide prevention speech ever made. Without it thousands, possibly millions, might have taken their own lives in the traditional suicidal act of saving face. *". . . It is according to the dictates of time and fate that we have resolved to pave the way for a grand peace for all the generations to come by enduring the unendurable and suffering what is insufferable."* The Japanese went on, in defeat, to victory that still resonates in the world of commerce and private lives.

Suicide can be a powerful statement. But I think it is most often a tragic one.

CHAPTER 10

Where Does It Hurt?
How Can I Help?

God enters through the wound.

—ROBERT BLY

JOURNAL ENTRY, OCTOBER 21, 1998

I have a Turkish rug in my entry hall, a kilim, it is called. Blue, violet, green and white, it is wonderfully woven. In one corner is a flaw, some of the strands wandering off in no particular direction. When I bought the rug, I was told there is always a flaw in Turkish rugs, a place where "the devils may escape." Since then I have heard this about the American Indian weavings as well, and about other crafts; in many crafts, people leave a plainly mistaken clue that lets the devils pass out of their work. I think this grief I am going through is acceptance of the wound in all its pain, of the devils leaving and of God entering.

So in every wound, in each mistake and source of pain, there is also the place where God gets in, as the devils get out.

I will accept the places of hurt, the difficulties, as the places also where evil can depart and the grace of God can enter; I will pray for God to come into the wounds that are here in my soul, knowing that only God's grace can put me together again into a new shape, a new life, a new healing.

". . . We decide reluctantly to fall again into pain and heartache—and live."

—DR. EDWIN SHNEIDMAN

In many of the books I read about suicide over the last ten years—*On Suicide: Great Writers on the Ultimate Question,* Geo Stone's *Suicide and Attempted Suicide,* as well as articles, pieces in newspapers and magazines, and all the studies that have come across my desk—the name of one man, Edwin Shneidman, has appeared more than any person except A. Alvarez.

Two books of Shneidman's have achieved a prominence on my shelves—*Comprehending Suicide,* his 2001 book, and *The Suicidal Mind,* which came out in 1996 and which I found in paperback in the suicide section of a small bookstore in Manhattan earlier this year. This section is a new phenomenon. When Clark died, there was no suicide section in the bookstore and I always felt I had to whisper when I asked the question. Faces would fall, eyes flick around the room averting their look from mine. Now, there has been some small progress.

There are many who have labored valiantly in the field of suicide prevention and the understanding of this illness, none more than Professor Edwin Shneidman, who is considered the father of the suicide prevention movement in the United States. Recently I reached out to friends who have contacts at UCLA, where Shneidman is Professor of Thanatology Emeritus. I got his number and called. Although Shneidman was eighty-five and had been ill, he answered the telephone briskly and clearly. I introduced myself and asked him how he was feeling.

"Somewhere between radiance and death!" was his cheery reply. I identified myself as best I could, and he asked what kind of music I sing and inquired if I were a sort of star.

"I do mostly concerts at places like Carnegie Hall, I make records, I do television shows," I replied, not really knowing what it would be best to say. I sing like Judy Collins, I wanted to say. Later he told me that he came to know and love my work.

"You must be a chanteuse, from what you are telling me," he said. I agreed that he was certainly as close as most people get to identifying my style. He asked me why I was writing a book, and, after I had told him, I said I felt, after reading so much of his work as though he had lit a candle for me in a dark night, as though I had struck gold.

Shneidman is the founder of the American Association of Suicidology. In the 1950s, he and his partner, Norman Farberow, were codirectors of the Los Angeles Suicide Prevention Center, and during the Johnson administration, he was chief of the Center for the Study of Suicide Prevention at the National Institute of Mental Health in Bethesda, Maryland. In the 1960s, he was chief of the Los Angeles County General Hospital.

He is the author and editor of several books on suicide and the author of 160 articles and essays. His book, *Deaths of Man*, was nominated for a National Book Award. Shneidman has been a dynamo in the field of the study of suicide.

He writes about suicide with compassion, ease, understanding, and a tone that I find both uplifting and enlightening. From my first introduction to Shneidman's writing, I was impressed by the professor's kind, compassionate, and direct discussions of suicide. It is the humanist voice in the man's writing that speaks to me most clearly. He seems to understand both the suicide and the survivor's pain and is quoted by most of the professionals who write about the last taboo. On being introduced at a meeting of the American Association of Suicide Ideology in Washington ten years ago, Shneidman was described by a colleague in the following manner. "As Freud is to the unconscious, so Shneidman is to suicide."

"I have a special talent for writing books," he said, surprised that I know so much about him. "I write dozens of books that people don't read and that don't sell." We laughed over this together, but I told him that I had read references to him in nearly every book I have ever read on suicide, and that his work and his passion for the subject was helping people all over the world.

"You have ploughed this path, and it will become a highway because of the work you have done," I told him.

Our talk turned into quite a conversation, and we exchanged some history. I told him about my son, and my marriage, and a little about the writing I am doing. Professor Shneidman told me he has four children, three of whom are physicians, and the fourth is a full colonel in the Army Corps. He also told me of his six grandchildren, including one grandson of whom he is particularly proud. He was married for fifty-five years to a woman he regards as the love and romance of his life, and who had died recently. I spoke of all the things he has said, and the books he has written that I have read. I asked him about his thoughts on suicide.

"It is a matter of overwhelming pain," he tells me, "of what I like to call 'Psychache.'" We spoke of one of the better known educational organizations that sponsors suicide studies, those who have lost loved ones, those trying to pair drug companies with the study of suicide.

"I have a nonaggression pact with most of the current suicide organizations." He said that in his quiet, less dramatic approach, he is up against "the drug companies that push their products with a total disregard of talk therapy, the shell game that goes on in discussion—you talk about suicide and they talk about depression. You can live a long, unhappy life with depression, but without the component of suicidology in your life, you are not going to take your life. The universities seem to trade precision for relevance. I like precision, but I *revere* relevance," he said. A man after my own heart.

Shneidman's writing, I told him, referring particularly to the book *The Suicidal Mind*, from 1996, in which he discusses the lives of five different suicides, is always easy and accessible.

"Do you know the phrase 'lingua franca'?" I said I didn't. "That means, writing the ordinary speech of wherever you are." "Well," I told him, "it communicates to me very well. I feel you are talking directly to me." He chuckled, and I liked his soft laughter, his sense of humor.

As I talked to Shneidman, I was reminded of the time I

spent with my first psychologist, Ralph Klein, whom I began seeing in New York a few months after I was released from National Jewish Hospital in Denver. I had been recovering from tuberculosis and getting my divorce proceedings in order, spending time with my son until his father spirited him back to Connecticut (kidnap, I think, but it was not illegal). Ralph Klein's territory for my treatment was manifold: I had a deep psychological problem in my situation with my son; I had made a serious attempt on my life; I drank; I was depressed; I was a young woman, twenty-four years old, with a new and very fragile career as a singer (I had made two albums and done a lot of singing in clubs and at festivals, but my success in the music business was far in the future). I had applied at the William Allyson White foundation for "free" therapy and seen someone there once or twice, I think, but when I met up with Ralph, I decided I would make the money for therapy no matter what, because Ralph was intelligent and sensitive, and smart.

Ralph was involved with the Sullivanians, a group named after Harry Stack Sullivan, the psychiatrist known for his theory of interpersonal relations. Jane Pearce and Saul Newton, cofounders of the Sullivan Institute for Research in Psychoanalysis, wrote a book about their beliefs called *Conditions of Human Growth*. There were strange ideas among the Sullivanians, for instance, that drink was a good thing for a nervous twenty-four-year-old, even though someone with knowledge in the field of alcoholism would have known that I had a serious problem with booze, even at twenty-four.

But the Sullivanians also had some wonderful ideas about human growth. Ralph taught me that making and keeping friends meant learning to be responsible about communication—to answer phone calls and make dates with people and be there for them. He taught me to keep journals, and to listen to my dreams and my visions for my music and my creativity. He taught me to respect my dreams and follow them; he helped me learn to do the work, and to close.

Professor Shneidman is a lot like Ralph. He has been there; he knows what he is talking about, having treated suicidal men and women, studied the subject as a scholar and a teacher, and written about the subject for nearly sixty years. Shneidman's message is so humanist, so pertinent, and his voice in regards to suicide is the voice of kindness, understanding, and healing.

"I would love to learn more about your life and your work in this field," I told him, "since I have become a sort of student of the subject, and of your work, because of my own loss."

"I'm used to students doing homework," he said, and I smiled to myself. He is like Max, my singing teacher, I thought, chuckling. I wanted to tell him how much of a student I really am, but refrained. I agreed to do some homework. He said he first wanted me to read his autobiography, which he would send me because it is out of print. We agreed to exchange books and thoughts. Professor Shneidman said as we hung up, "You are an angel dropped from heaven." I smiled, sure that I had visited, as well, with an angel.

I put together a bunch of things—CDs, so he can hear the "chanteuse," my book *Singing Lessons,* and some other things, photographs and the like. In the mail next day, via FedEx (this guy may be eighty-five, but he is sharp as a tack!), is a large envelope of material from the professor. On the flyleaf of the materials—in his handwriting:

— For your delectation
— We'll talk

And I begin, with fascination and pleasure, to read. In his 1989 biography, *A Life and Death: Notes of a Committed Suicidologist*, Shneidman tells of his beloved family who gave him, in his "happy, tepid home," nothing to recoil against.

"The result [of my happy childhood] was no heroic dichotomies, no tragic bifurcations, no searing divorcements, no painful self-exiling . . . against which to overreact and pit one's life. [At that time, he adds, there were no Hitlers.] One simply cannot become a great thinker or writer on an uncracked foundation like that." Therefore, he calls himself an "iconoclast within the temple."

Shneidman breathes humanity and understanding into his writing about suicide, and says things that are perhaps unpopular, but ring with truth, usefulness, and insight to me and many others.

For instance: "I know that the current fetish is to have the appearance of precision—and the kudos and vast monies that often go with it—and that is not my style. Nowadays, the gambit used to make a field appear scientific is to redefine what is being discussed. The most flagrant current example is to convert the study of suicide, almost by sleight of hand, into a discussion of depression—two very different things." Shneidman continues: "I beleve that suicide is essentially a drama in the mind, where the suicidal drama is almost always driven by psychological pain, the pain of negative emotions—what I call 'psychache.' Psychache is at the main root of suicide; no psychache, no suicide."

In his paper, "This I Believe," Shneidman says:

"We need to give back to introspection the good name that it had before the nineteenth-century psychologists Wundt and Titchner ponderously trivialized it. Each suicide has its own unrepeatable anguish and special logic; the mischief lives in that innocent word 'therefore,' as in 'therefore I must kill myself.' . . . I believe that suicide is a function of the mind. The mind—has a mind of its own. The main business of the mind is to mind its own business."

I remember the admonition, from the alcoholism rehab I went to, that one should "not buy into your own soap opera," not let the dramatics of your mind rule you. Think a drink through, they would say. Think the suicide through, I would later think. "Feelings aren't facts." I have had to teach my mind to mind its own business, just as Shneidman suggests.

"Suicide is often less a decision than a reaction," Shneidman says. He, who coined the term "Suicidology," began his work on suicide in 1949 in Los Angeles. He was studying the self-inflicted deaths of two patients at a VA hospital in Brentwood, reading their suicide notes and becoming, he says, mesmerized by their decisions. The study catapulted him into a lifetime study of suicide and its causes. His early writings on the causes of suicide were more personal in nature than his later findings. Then, he pondered the idea that "suicide [might be] the result of thwarted love, shattered control, assaulted self-image, grief, and rage."

"It is almost as though the suicidal drama was autonomously writing itself, as though the play had a mind of its own."

Shneidman is a stickler for the truth. Referring to the increasing numbers of suicides around the world, Schneidman has said:

. . . It has to sober us to realize that as long as people, consciously or unconsciously, can successfully dissemble, no suicide prevention program can be a hundred percent successful.

Secrets, we know, can kill. The secrecy surrounding the suicide can kill the survivors. I always lied about how much I drank. Hence, my depression. Alcohol is a depressant, so drinking while medicating my depression could have put me into another—probably successful—suicide attempt, since statistics show that alcoholics who are drinking are frequently successful at committing suicide.

Shneidman sounds a strong note of warning against the secrecy that surrounds this most "dreadful" and "awful" act, which perpetrates what I personally see as an illness in itself—secrecy—whose effect on the family survivors after a completed suicide is more toxic than poison.

Unlike most doctors and professionals in the field today, Shneidman does not think that drugs are always the answer for people with the suicide illness, or ideology, as he calls it. While not opposed to drug therapies, Schneidman thinks the so-called biologicalization of suicide is simplistic.

"It treats the symptoms, not the disorder . . . doesn't ignore the external connections: religion, family, work. Each suicide is 'sui generic.' Its reasons, like the mind itself, cannot be categorized. Clinical labels are specious and to build a profession on them is to put a skyscraper on sandy soil."

Professor Shneidman's twin passions are suicide and Herman Melville. He keeps a copy of *Moby-Dick* on his desk and is said to refer often to its opening paragraphs, the same words my father read to me so many years ago on that bright shining day in Denver, before I knew anything about suicide: *"Whenever I find myself growing grim about the mouth; whenever it is a damp, drizzly November in my soul . . ."*

I am sure Shneidman knows that Melville's son took his own life. I wonder if my father ever knew.

Edwin Shneidman says one of the three areas of real difficulty for people with suicidology is the lack of a good relationship with the father. He does not distinguish whether it is the male or the female child who is at risk because of lacking a good relationship with the father. (Nancy Friday's proposal in *My Mother, Myself* is that the female child must have a good relationship with the mother to mature in a steady and healthy way. I must look in her book to see if she talks about suicide.) The other two areas of great risk, Shneidman has concluded after studying suicides and their histories for sixty years, are those of work and satisfaction in work, and the spouse, or the person we might call the partner today.

Professor Shneidman says psychache is at the dark heart of suicide; no psychache, no suicide. And two questions that are at the heart of treating someone who wishes to end their life are:

"Where does it hurt?"

And "How can I help you?"

CHAPTER II

Youth, Light, *and* Memory

Death ends a life, but it does not end a relationship, which struggles on in the survivor's mind towards some resolution which it may never find.

—GILBERT CATES

. . . Only the present is eternal—all things having a past and a future are doomed to pass away . . .

—THOMAS MERTON, *THE INTIMATE MERTON: HIS LIFE FROM HIS JOURNALS*

JOURNAL ENTRY, MAY 14, 1994

In the early sixties I met a Native American woman named Maria Mendez. Maria was my hospital floormate at National Jewish Hospital for Tuberculosis in Denver. Maria came to my concert this week in Montana.

She brought me beautiful beadwork that she has done for me, and told me about what has happened to her in these many years since we have seen each other last. She is very excited about being at my concert here in Billings. I feel quite emotional seeing Maria; it is as though my youth and my present life have somehow merged in time. I ask her if I sang at the hospital.

"Yes, you sang for us." Maria has asthma, as I do, perhaps a natural development from the lung problems we suffered from early in our lives. She is an activist and has been all over the world, to China, to Vietnam. She is a bright, beautiful woman, filled with spirit. She tells me that after she left the hospital, she went back to the Cheyenne tribe in Lame Deer, Montana, where she lives now, with her Apache husband, five sons, and two daughters. I tell her I am happy for her.

"You were in deep pain in Denver because of the separation from your husband, and the custody of your son," she says.

"My son took his own life last year," I tell her.

"I know that. It makes me so sad. I want you to come to Lame Deer Reservation. I will share my sons with you." I am suddenly in tears, sobbing in Maria's arms. There is no way to live through this loss but to feel it, to experience the loss over and over.

I pray I will wake someday to find you here with me again. I will go the Cheyenne and watch Maria's sons dance for you and me.

When I was nineteen, and pregnant, my father and I were very close, and my mother and I had become distanced. This was due in great part to my father's attempts monopolize me (and everyone else), soaking up the attention as he did, because he was dramatic and took up more than the usual emotional space. It didn't leave enough room for my relationship with my mother to grow.

Mother wrote to me in Boulder, where I was living with my first husband, Peter Taylor, and pregnant—very pregnant!—with Clark. I don't have the letter anymore, unfortunately, but in it she said that she needed to be with me, to tear down the fence that both of us knew my father had tried to erect between us. She suggested I drive down to Denver and have lunch with her.

I once described the letter and the subsequent lunch to three women with whom I was doing a television interview that focused on successful women's relationships with their mothers—both good and bad. These women— Whoopi Goldberg, Estelle Parsons, and my very close friend Susan Cheever, who had had very different experiences with their mothers—were amazed at my mother's bravery, her directness, and her success at having regained, over a lunch on that September afternoon when I was pregnant and ready to listen, not only my trust, but my undying friendship and enduring love. I am sure I always loved my mother anyway, but as I explained, that lunch with her sealed our friendship and probably saved my sanity in the years to come.

I drove down to Denver and picked Mom up at the house on Marion and we drove to a restaurant in Cherry Creek, an upscale shopping mall near the house. We both ordered Manhattans and drank them while we ate, and ordered more Manhattans and talked and talked. We loosened up together, not for the first time, but this was different—we were telling the truth about things we had felt and hurts we had harbored. We talked about Daddy and his philandering and about the pain of his being unfaithful to mother. She told me her story, of falling in love with Daddy on the rebound at twenty-two, of how she had been smitten by my father, and had always forgiven him his trespasses and had never been unfaithful to him. I had to ask her again to be sure, but of course, I knew she had always been there with us, for us, whether Daddy had come home on time or not—cooking, sewing, cleaning, reading to us, taking us to music lessons and school and the dentist and the doctor (we didn't often go to the doctor, but when we did, she took us). When in the world would she ever have had time for an affair? That didn't surprise me, but hearing her say that she had always forgiven him and never betrayed him touched me in a deep way.

It had taken courage for my mother to marry a blind man, talented as he was. It took courage for her to raise five children ("six," she would say, "including your father"), and it took courage to stay in the marriage while Daddy was doing whatever Daddy did. She had stayed with him through thick and thin. It was because she loved him.

We were fast friends from that moment on, a moment that grew into years. That day long ago in Denver, we talked with total honesty, clarity, and humor, long past the lunch hour and into the afternoon, while the light from a winter sun shifted between the red curtains in the windows and the staff in the restaurant stood about, idle and restless, waiting for us to leave. We were both drunk enough by the time we left that somebody else should have been the designated driver, but somehow I got in my station wagon and made it back to Boulder intact, and she got back to the house on Marion. I will never forget the experience, or my mother's bravery.

Today my mother is eighty-seven, and full of life, love of her husband (my stepfather, Robert), her family, five children, seven grandchildren, and one great-grandchild. She is still beautiful and dresses well, often in outfits I and my sister Holly covet, sometimes in jewels and scarves and skirts we give her. She has great taste in clothes, collects owls, which we all send her from all over the world, owls from Steuben and Coleport and Baccarat, owls made of glass, bone, steel, clay, paper, silk, and stone. The wise eyes of hundreds of little creatures stare out of the exhibit cases in which mother now keeps them, others roam every surface of her home in Denver. She has recently said she is done with collecting them, but every time I see a diamond or a jeweled owl, or a T-shirt with an owl on it, or an etching or painting of an owl, I reach out for it, thinking it would be perfect for my mother, the wisest of all owls.

Mom belongs to a book club that meets every Monday morning, and I don't think she has missed very many of those meetings in the thirty years she has been a member. It is a very exclusive book club that started in her church thirty years ago, and someone has to die for a new member to get in. My mother treasures the club and the reading the group does together. They go into depth with South American Literature, or perhaps the writing of the pioneer movements, women's journals and fiction written on the treks from Missouri to the Pacific, from the Midwest to the mountain states. She is an avid reader but this club has focused her reading, and prompted in-depth research; last year, when the club read all of *Remembrance of Things Past*, my mother did a paper on the Dreyfus case in French history, going to the library to take out rare books about the case, whose anti-Semitic roots still reverberate through French history, and whose story forms part of Proust's great novel of remembrance.

My mother is a Unitarian, and she and my stepfather, Robert, go camping almost every weekend in the summer with about ninety other Unitarians. I like to tell her the joke about the time somebody burned a question mark on the lawn of a Unitarian's house. Robert used to be a school principal in Colorado and was school superintendent for years, and he and my Mom have seen most of Colorado, every campground and lake, most mountain ranges and rivers. On their weekend camping trips in the summer, traveling in their third camper, they venture out into the wilderness with their Unitarian friends, with whom they have long and enduring friendships. During the week, there are "sip and sups," and Mother and Robert prepare chili relenos and fudge, roasted turkey and stuffing, salads of nuts and oranges, sweet and sour dressings, molded Jell-O, taking them to progressive dinners that fill many of their nights. They play bridge and go to the theater and to the symphony, and take turns driving thousands of miles to visit their children (Robert has five kids, as does my mom). Often when I call the house in Denver, I have to leave a message—they are out to dinner, the theater, with friends, seeing a movie, gallivanting, as I say to Mom, all over the city. Sometimes I think their social and family life surpasses mine. All of her children are dazzled by my mother's liveliness, her intense relationship with politics and her children, and the world around her. My mother and father taught me that it is my job in life to make a difference, and my mother is the best model, making her world and her family and her community a better place to be.

Mom is funny, and finds humor in many things. We laugh on the phone, and every time I cook a turkey, I have to call her to find out how many minutes to cook the bird, whether to put it in a hot or a cool oven, whether to sauté till totally soft or keep the celery and onions crisp. I know perfectly well how to cook a turkey, but my conversation with my mother about these things is much more important than the finished bird in the oven.

My mother was there for me when Clark died. She met up with me on the road and traveled with me in Billings, Montana, where as a little girl I rode in the backseat of the Buick, while my mother drove my father through the west to do his shows. She was there for me, as she always had been, even when I didn't notice.

I am so lucky that my mother has turned out to be my close friend, someone I can talk to about everything, the family, politics, food, books, anything that is going on in my life. She is wise, like her beloved owls. She has a bright, eager mind, and she is an inspiration to me and her other children. That is about as good as it could get, and I got it. I am one lucky daughter.

CHAPTER 12

Children *of* Jonah *and* Socrates

Carefully planned acts of suicide are as rare as carefully planned acts of homicide.

—GEO STONE

It takes a tremendous amount of energy to figure out how you're going to kill yourself. I wanted something that was final and wasn't going to be messy, I didn't want to jump off the roof; I might end up only half dead, and I wouldn't like that. I didn't want to blow my head off—I didn't happen to feel that physical disembodiment would be a particularly pleasant thing for everybody. . . . I kept thinking about what would be the easiest for everyone else.

Of course the easiest thing would have been if I had lived.

—GEO STONE

. . .

Are people who kill themselves crazy?

"Yes, no, not necessarily, and so what?" Geo Stone answers, in his wonderfully researched and thorough book, *Suicide and Attempted Suicide*, published in 1999. Stone says we are more likely, here in the United States, to take our own lives than to be murdered. Today, there are psycho-pharmacologists who prescribe antidepressants and other drugs for their patients with increasing regularity. There is not time, many of them feel, for the "outdated" manner of psychotherapy. And anyway, they want to speed their patients along. Speaking of therapy as opposed to drugs, Geo Stone says, "Lest the antipsychiatry crowd get too smug, note that some antidepressant drugs seem to increase suicidal behavior, as do some tranquilizers." How many times have you heard, after someone has taken his own life, "they were changing his medication, it was not working."

I am convinced by my own experience, as well as documented evidence from alcoholism studies that alcohol and drugs are a leading cause of suicide. But many suicides are not researched as to their drug- and alcohol-related issues. I would venture a large bet that many suicides are fueled by alcohol and/ or drugs.

Suicide can be alluring, compelling, seductive, driven by chemical dependency, mental illness, depression, and fear. In many times and cultures in history, it has been considered illegal. A. Alvarez, in his book, *The Savage God*, tells of a man who was hanged for unsuccessfully trying to kill himself by slitting his throat. Alvarez also calls suicide a "closed world with its own irresistible logic." For those of us who have gone there and come back from the edge of the precipice, it is also the great mystery. Why others and not us? Why did a friend of mine try twenty-five times to take her own life when she was drinking and never try again when she was sober, and why did my son, who was drinking at the time, succeed in taking his own life on his third try? (I think it was only his third.)

With suicide, there is also always the question of the power and the honor of choice. If I don't have the choice to select the time when I depart this life, I have no real personal freedom, which is at the root of self-determination. I have the right, if I choose, to end my life. The problem with most of us, who are young and healthy in most respects, except for those suffering from mental illness and addiction and the depression disease, is that we don't usually really choose. The substance chooses for us, perhaps alcohol or drugs, legal and illegal; or, the untreated depression chooses. We don't choose, in most cases, though we would like to think we do. Often, our self-determination is an illusion. Other forces, powerful, seductive, negative, and often treatable with talking therapy as well as the new antidepressant drugs, are in control. For centuries, suicides have had to deal with the condemnation of the church and state. Only recently have insurance companies started to pay out on policies after a suicide. But there are still many taboos related to suicide.

Survivors must often bear pain and such indignity, and often, the memory of the loved one, the one who has gone by way of his or her own hand, is layered over with mystery and myth, sorrow and unkindness, misunderstanding and, often, unintentional and even calculated cruelty. As a survivor, I swore that I would try to break those bonds of the taboo and speak out for myself and for my son, as well as for other survivors of this sorrowful loss.

How do we put the taboos to rest finally, relinquish our punishment of the suicide and his or her family, and realize that understanding, compassion, and medical treatment in the form of therapies and appropriate drugs are the way of knowledge and must be applied to the treatment of this disease? For it is a disease, the depression disease, or, as Shneidman says, the psych-ache, that leads to the urge to take one's own life.

Every eighteen minutes someone in the United States kills themselves. A few are younger than ten years old; others are over ninety. Between 7.5 and 16 percent take more than a day to die. An estimated 300,000 to 600,000 survive suicide attempts, but suffer varying degrees of injury; 19,000 are permanently disabled each year.

Only about one in ten to twenty suicide attempts is fatal. In his thorough book, *Suicide and Attempted Suicide,* Geo Stone wants those who contemplate suicide to understand what they are dealing with, and to make decisions that are enlightened with knowledge of the methods and their success or failure. Of course, knowledge and enlightenment seem to contradict the state of mind of the suicide. I am sure Clark did not think his death through. He was upset on his death tape that this event was taking so very long. He could not have planned well. He knew too little, or perhaps too much. Stone wants to let people know that the decision to end their life should be their own, and is usually due to temporary problems; therefore most suicides are tragic mistakes.

How could I not agree with Stone? He is convinced that people through the centuries have been determined, if they are going to take their lives, no matter whether they have appropriate means at hand or not. And the problem, as he sees it, is that to get the information one might need to complete a successful (and presumably, psychologically and physically painless) suicide, one should have as much information as possible, which is practically impossible, because, as we have seen, discussion of suicide is largely a taboo. He goes on to place suicide attempters in one of four groups: (1) Rational people facing an insoluble problem, generally a fatal or debilitating illness; (2) impulsive people, frequently young, truly but temporarily miserable, often *drunk* (my italics), who wouldn't even consider suicide six months later; (3) irrational people, often *alcoholic* (my italics), schizophrenic, or depressed; (4) desperate people, people trying to make a safe gesture as a cry for help or to get someone's attention.

Here is his list of the methods people have used over the centuries, put aside in a note to the first chapter of Geo Stone's book, setting the tone of suicide's history:

> *In the absence of knowledge about suicide methods—and alternatives to suicide—people will continue to act in desperation and ignorance, as they have throughout recorded history, with a gun, rope, blade, poison, and anything else available. That is the reality. To give you some idea, over the past two centuries people have committed suicide by jumping into volcanoes, vats of beer, crocks of vinegar, retorts of molten glass, white-hot coke ovens, or slaughterhouse tanks of blood; by throwing themselves upon buzz saws; by thrusting hot pokers down their throats; by suffocating in refrigerators or chimneys; by locking themselves into high-altitude test chambers; by crashing airplanes; by jumping from airplanes; by lying in front of steamrollers; by throwing*

themselves into the third (high voltage) rail; by touching high-tension wires; by placing their necks in vises and turning the handle; by hugging stoves; by freezing to death; by climbing into lions' cages; by blowing themselves up with cannons, hand grenades or dynamite; by boring holes in their heads with power drills; by drinking hydrochloric acid or Drāno; by walking in front of cars, trains, subways and racehorses; by driving cars off cliffs or into trains; by swallowing poisonous spiders; by piercing their hearts with corkscrews or darning needles; by starving themselves; by swallowing underwear; by stabbing themselves with spectacles sharpened to a point; by cutting their throats with handsaws, sheep shears, or barbed wire; by forcing teams of horses to tear their heads off; by decapitating themselves with homemade guillotines; by exposing themselves to swarms of bees; by injecting themselves with paraffin, cooking oil, peanut butter, mercury, deodorant, or mayonnaise; by crucifying themselves; by swallowing coins; by swallowing cruci-fixes; by cutting their wrist with their teeth; by cutting off their arm with a kitchen knife; by stuffing rags into their mouth and pebbles up their nose; by exploding a stick of dynamite in their mouth; by sawing their skull with a band saw; by inhaling tal-cum powder; by injecting themselves with HIV-positive blood.

The methods people use, all too often leave them neither dead, nor fully recovered, but maimed and permanently in-jured: paralyzed from jumps, brain-damaged from gunshots, comatose from drugs . . . For anyone considering suicide (or even "safe" suicide gestures; nothing is 100 percent reliable), I urge you to try every alternative first—and then try them again."

My sister, Holly, sent me a book called *On Suicide: Great Writers on the Ultimate Question*, which came out in 1992. A section from Howard Kushner's book, *Self-Destruction in the Promise Land*, is included in this book. In it, Kushner, professor of history at San Diego State University, discusses Meriweather Lewis and Abraham Lincoln and the reasons for the success of one's suicide attempt and the failure of the other's. At the beginning of the piece, he talked about Max White, who took his life in 1893. He was nineteen and shot himself in a canyon outside of San Diego while hunting. Max White was a Hungarian émigré, hoping for a position for which he had not been hired. This was a time of economic depression in the United States, and he was despondent over not finding work.

> . . . *Max White was only one of many suicides reported by American newspapers in 1893 . . . Several months before White's death, the editors of the* San Diego Union, *fearing a suicide epidemic, published a long editorial warning that "suicide has become so frequent as to attract little attention. Day after day the rehearsal of these crimes goes on in the daily press, and,"* the Union *feared, "the horror which such acts should produce is giving way to indifference, or a morbid condition of the public mind which accepts self-murder as excusable and the natural outgrowth of modern conditions of life.*

The view of the *San Diego Union* paper was mirrored in the writing in the same time period of a French moral statistician, Emil Durkheim (1858–1917), who, in his book, *Suicide: A Study in Sociology*, offered the reason for the epidemic: "modern life was the killer." He outlined four major types of suicide—egoistic, altruistic, anomic, and fatalistic—and concentrated primarily in the study of two of these—the egoistic and the anomic suicides. Kushner quotes Durkheim as explaining that anomie "throws open the door to disillusionment and consequently to disappointment . . . very many of these suicides expressed primarily irritation and exasperated weariness. Sometimes they contain blasphemies, violent recriminations against life in general, sometimes threats and accusations against a particular person to whom the responsibility for the suicide's unhappiness is imputed."

In his article, Kushner quotes Freud as having believed that suicide always contains an earlier repressed desire to kill someone else: "No neurotic harbors thoughts of suicide which he has not turned back upon himself from murderous impulses against others."

That would concur with my own feelings of rage against my father for his asking me to do something I could not do. I certainly would not have been capable of articulating the desire to murder my father—I knew too much about the Greek myths, how children who murder their parents are doomed to a much worse fate than taking their own lives might bring down upon them. I didn't know then that suicide and homicide bring similar casts of darkness with them.

In Emil Durkheim's view, people can be both homicidal and suicidal. It seems strange that a person who can blame others, in his suicide note, or in his predisposition to suicide and the tone of a life of reaction to others, chooses to take his or her *own life* as a revenge. Kushner tells us in his article that "[Max]

White's diary and suicide note provided ample evidence of his profound sense of unresolved loss . . . [he] had many legitimate complaints . . . and he coupled his own suicide with threats of revenge against those he imagined had plotted his unhappy fate."

Many famous suicides have lashed out in homicide against others before taking their own lives. In recent memory, the young shooters at the Columbine massacre in Englewood, Colorado, took their own lives after killing many of their peers. In some articles about these disturbed, twisted boys at Columbine, whose pathology destroyed their classmates as well as their own lives, it seems they are hungry for some action to show their disdain and disgust for what passes as life in Englewood, Colorado, and the fact that other children have more, or different, things in their lives. Jealousy. Much of their behavior, from what I have read, came as a result of the use of mood-changing drugs. Others say they acted because they were ill—mentally ill, perhaps predisposed to the anomic syndrome that Durkheim spotted, dissatisfaction with life on life's terms.

In another story in the collection *On Suicide*, in which I later found this moving piece by Kushner, the writer Walker Percy describes his father's suicide, which he witnessed.

"Why did he want me to be there? To show me what? Now I know. To show me the one sure sweet exodus." His father had at first arranged his death to look like an accident: "But the second shot was a double shot aimed at [me]. I thought he missed me and he did, almost, and I thought I survived and I did, almost. But now I have learned something and been surprised by it, after all. [My father] killed me then and I did not know it. I have been living, yes, but it is a living death because I knew [my father] wanted me dead . . . I am alive . . . like the sole survivor of Treblinka, who lived by a fluke, but did not really feel entitled to live."

In his piece on the suicide of Meriweather Lewis, who was beset by debts and unhappiness after his fame as the Explorer of the West with his partner, William Clark, Kushner quotes Jefferson, who was a close friend of Lewis's and had known him since childhood, as saying Lewis's suicide was a result of "a constitutional disposition to depressions of the mind" that was "inherited by him from his father." Knowing little about the genetics of the source of depressions, alcoholism, bipolar disorders, and other conditions of which we in the twenty-first century have been accustomed to hearing, it is remarkable that Jefferson himself could draw this conclusion. The apple, as they say, doesn't fall far from the tree. His father had it, too, Jefferson was saying. It is not so mysterious.

Lewis's enemy, Louisiana Territorial Secretary Frederick Bates, who had refused to pay certain bills that the government claimed were not valid, attributed the explorer's suicide to insanity. "Mental derangement," he insisted, was at the root of both Lewis's political miscarriages and his subsequent suicide.

I believe suicide is ultimately a question of the state of our souls. For me, the mental health that will lead me away from self-murder (by little or big doses) starts and ends with the soul.

According to many recent statistics I have read about suicide, there are approximately 600,000 people who try to take their own lives in this country each year. And according to Sharon Rose Blauner, whose book, *How I Stayed Alive When My Brain Was Trying to Kill Me*, came out in 2002, the figure is even higher—750,000. The *Los Angeles Times*, in a May 2002 article about suicide, says that most of the self-inflicted wounds of people who find their way to emergency rooms are the result of failed suicide attempts. If hundreds of thousands of people in America try to kill themselves every year, as the statistics tell us, then since the publication of Alvarez's book, 18 million Americans can also call themselves failed suicides. I myself am a failed suicide. Since I tried to take my own life in 1954, there may be as many as 30 million of us running around the country, having outlived our darkest nights. And that is just in the United States. The suicide rates in the rest of the world are equally as staggering.

A. Alvarez, who wrote *The Savage God: A Study of Suicide*, also calls himself a failed suicide. His book, published in 1971, is a study of the life and death of the Italian writer Cesare Pavese, as well as poet Sylvia Plath, and a reflection on the author's own attempt to end his life. Alvarez speaks of suicide as "a closed world . . . with its own irresistible and fatal logic. So—be careful not to kill all your demons, for in their mystery lies the possibility for beauty, for inspiration, as well as for darkness and death. "What a problem for the troubled soul!

Alvarez wrote:

> *As for suicide: the sociologists and psychologists who talk of it as a disease puzzle me now as much as the Catholics and Muslims who call it the most deadly or mortal of sins. It seems to me to be . . . a terrible but utterly natural reaction to the strained, narrow, unnatural necessities we sometimes create for ourselves.*

For me, that translates into no plan B.

Max White's invocation to his enemies embodies many of the feelings of those whose answer to life's problems is to take their own lives:

> *Ah, you false friends, who with your mouth claimed your friendship and with your hands withheld it! My curse upon you. May you ever feel misfortune blighting your whole career. My hatred is indescribable against you.*

Max White did not kill others, only himself. But he did not intend his enemies to go unpunished. His curses followed them to whatever fate might await them. I read his note as a death curse on the heads of those he considered his enemies.

Durkheim "accepts self-murder as excusable and the natural outgrowth of modern conditions of life."

Still, as Geo Stone says, "How do you know that suicide is the answer if you haven't tried everything else first? *You can always kill yourself later.*"

CHAPTER 13

Love *and* Power

The light that I see is not localized,
but it is far brighter than a cloud
which surrounds the sun
—I call it "the shadow of the living light."

—HILDEGARD OF BINGEN

JOURNAL ENTRY, SEPTEMBER 20, 1996

I know that we see through a glass darkly now, but later we will see things clearly, like the sun.

One night my brother, Denver, comes to dinner and brings me a book about the women who wrote and studied in the convents during the Middle Ages. I am lifted in reading of their journeys, these women who, in the world outside their cloistered walls, would have had little chance for education and for learning. In making their covenant with Christ and following the calling of the veil, they are given the opportunity to study, learn languages, work on the illumination of manuscripts, refine their love of Christ, and do the service of prayer for the world suffering outside. They were lights in the darkness of cruelty and destruction that surrounded them in heathen wars, in the fight for territory, the greed for power. They studied, they prayed, they meditated upon forgiveness of sins, for the world outside, and for themselves.

Hildegard speaks of the light, the same light that surrounds me in the suffering world of today. The planet is still a place of pain, as it was in the dark ages. But I am making my own way toward that bright light of hope, that light of love, centuries later, and my journey, so different from that of Hildegard, or of other women in history, is not so different after all. We are all looking for the light and hope and peace.

I will meditate upon that light that shines from the past into the present, from old pain to new pain, healing today as it did in days of ancient prayer. Forever new, forever bright, it is the light of love and power, the light of hope.

About two months after Clark's death, when the notes and the calls and the letters and the visits of loving friends and strangers had slowed down, when others started thinking I would be wise to let it go, stop talking about it, get on with my life (some actually said this to me—not just with eye or body language, but with words—that it was time I stopped reciting my loss to myself, or anyone else.), I started sleeping late. Then, later. Then, late enough that it scared me. I went to therapy, and I talked. I talked to everyone who would listen about my son's death. I told my then therapist that I was terribly depressed and asked him if I should be in therapy, and he told me he thought that I was doing all right, that I was walking through this terrible new landscape, and that if I couldn't walk the grid, as he put it, then we would talk about medication.

I talked to friends, I talked to my doctors, and I talked to the woman who cleaned my room in Cincinnati, a black woman who slowly mopped the bathroom floor while I stood putting on my makeup in a room that faced a river. I don't know if she heard me, but she nodded sympathetically and seemed to comprehend completely. She said nothing but looked at me with what seemed like understanding. She moved around the room, her big, soft, padded form in her print shirt and blue skirt polishing the tabletops, mopping the floors, straightening the magazines on the tabletop, and she nodded, and murmured, and said yes, I understand.

"I understand" is the most powerful phrase in the language.

The language of the heart.

I went to spiritual meetings at church and shared about Clark. Some knew him, having met him or heard me talk of him through the years, knew he had succeeded in ending his life. They were concerned that I would not make it.

How do you make it? And have I made it? Today, yes, but there are no guarantees. Tomorrow, I don't know about.

I only know about today.

I try to get as much sleep as possible. I meditate as regularly as I can, trying to do this every day, and I focus on what is positive in my life. I found that eating sugar wasn't such a good idea at first, so I didn't, and then I did, eating sugar and loving it from time to time. There seemed to be rules, firm and rigid, and then there seemed to be no rules at all, except about drinking. I don't drink, and tell myself that I won't, not if my ass falls off. My ass has fallen off, and thank God, I didn't drink. I read that using pills and alcohol blurs the recovery stage, anyway. I wanted to be present, though the pain was devastating. I wanted to go through it, hoping that if I did it all with total clarity, I wouldn't have to do it again. Of course, I couldn't know that the pain, the reality, never changes—it will always be there, the hole that was in the place where my son, or at least his physical presence, had been.

For a few years I was playing around with a lyric I finished in 1995.

Wind, Water, Fire, and Stone

A dream came to me at night
When the boats were in the sea
A dream of the Black Death of earth
Two voices came singing to me.

> *Wind, water, fire, and stone.*
> *Storms of sand, closing over the sun*
> *Sand, fire, water, and wind*
> *How can we begin again.*

But you can't sink a rainbow
In a world that is green

You can't make the night any brighter
By even one star.

    Awake, awake, awake.

Oh the rivers are poisoned
And the lakes are gone
The dolphins are dying
And the whales have lost their song.

But you can't sink a rainbow
In a world that is green
You can't make the night any brighter

    Awake, awake, awake.

By even one star.

    Awake, awake, awake.

Once I saw a man
Who said he'd seen a flock of nightingales
Once a child recalled the sound of rain
Like silver angel's wings.

Like a lost and homeless thing
The planet spins her way through space.
Drugged and battered like a woman
Who can't recall her face.

Remembering the way she used to shine
Rivers in the sea
Shine, herons on the wing,
And hear the crickets sing
A million forest birds
The sea her mantle green
Like a banner of bright hair
Around her shoulders

But you can't sink a rainbow
In a world that is green
You can't make the world any brighter
By even one star.

    Awake, awake, awake.

A dream came to me at night
When the boats were in the sea
A dream of the bright death of earth.

CHAPTER 14

Blood *from the* Heart

*No one ever learned or achieved anything worth having
without being stretched beyond themselves, till their bones
crack . . . Every little step forward is made of sweat and
mutiny. Until the insight is won, until the craft is mastered.*

—GEORGE STEINER

JOURNAL ENTRY, 1993

These lessons are so hard. I don't want to bend on
some days, I won't stretch, my resistance says: I will
stay here, where I have come, this far and no farther.

But the pain is too much, the feelings are too strong,
the ache is too fierce. It is either move forward, or break. It
is either share this heavy load, with a friend, with a therapist, with a group, in my writing, in my music, or die.
Sometimes it is just that simple. If I have to stay here, not
climbing out further on the limb, not exercising once again

the aching muscles, I will evaporate, disappear, be no more, and fall apart.

I was at a party last night where I didn't talk about your death. There are many days now when I do, but once in a while I don't. But you were with me, and I thought about you, thought about how you would have loved the people I was with, people whose minds crackled and sparkled, for it was one of those places people were talking of change and energy and history, and I would have loved to have had you by my side, or filled you in afterward, describing every gesture, every joke, every dish served at a golden and crystal placing. You were with me, and though I referred to you once, speaking your name to someone who knows you are gone, I know I live by faith now, and the habit of keeping you in my heart at all times. Afterward we walked by your church, and I thought of you there, being christened. I felt your arms around me; I felt your love in my heart. I pray your love will help me survive this catastrophe.

Today is the tenth anniversary of my son's death.

A lot has changed, I am happier. I see the world not only as a place of loss, but of beauty and terror. What a mystery. I accept the terror and appreciate the beauty. I am grateful, counting my blessings. I am writing this morning, first going deep into the sorrow of my loss, then drifting in the reverie of joy. Funny that we are able to do both. But we are human. No behavior is foreign to us, for we might do anything that any man, any woman might do.

I am in my bedroom, which is also partly my writing studio. Around me in my room are my paperweights. They are spread out on a white radiator cover, along with amethyst geodes, statues of St. Francis and the Buddhas from Vietnam; a ceramic tile made by Picasso, a bright, eager face that greets me each morning; a vanilla-scented candle from Bombay is burning in a blue and white bowl; a bronze walking Buddha, one hand raised in benediction to serenity and surrender; my mother's needlepoint Chagall squares of the stained-glass windows at St. Paul de Vence hang on the walls along with a Wyoming oil painting by my sister, Holly, a bunch of flowers by Louis, and a vivid green and blue painting by my friend Esteban Vicente, who painted until he died at ninety-seven last year. There are copies of Tiffany lamps (and a real one somewhere in the apartment), watercolors of mine and Louis's that we have done at Caneel Bay, in the mountains of Colorado, at the beach, in the country. My two doctoral hoods hang together, one primarily green and one purple, one a doctorate in humane letters from Hobart and William Smith College and one from the New School University in New York. There are books of every kind on the bookshelves—history, fiction, memoir—signed books from Susan Cheever and Judy Chicago, Gay Talese and Carl Bernstein and poet Robert Pinsky—and a long row of books about suicide, in the order in which they came into my life after Clark's death.

Silent Grief: Living in the Wake of Suicide, by Christopher Lukas and Henry M. Seiden, was the book that was sent to us by Claire and Sherwin Kaufman, who lost their son to suicide a few years before Clark's death. I remember sitting in the living room of our apartment in New York while the late January sun poured through the windows and my tears fell on the pages. I had not seen anything in print that spoke to my pain before. I read and reread this book. Lukas and Seiden described what they called the First Wave of emotions—

I didn't know where to turn. I didn't know what was happening to me. I didn't believe it. I refused *to believe it. Thank God it wasn't me! How could he leave me like this?*

I was so relieved to finally hear people speak of what they were feeling about suicide. One father refused to even think about it. "It is not my problem," was his answer. Or, as I later read in Sue Chance's book about her son, Jim, "the only one with blood on his hands is Jim." Sue's book, *Stronger than Death: When Suicide Touches Your Life,* came out later that year, and I read with such compassion the story of her son's death. The journals, the self-searching, the growing understanding that she couldn't have prevented her son's death, just as my friend-to-be, Iris Bolton, spoke of powerlessness in her book about her own son. There was nowhere to go, I began to understand, but inside. Recovery from suicide is an inside job.

I pulled out *The Savage God,* by A. Alvarez, about that time. I had bought the book when it first came out ten years before, out of intellectual curiosity, but had no heart to read it, as though putting off the reading of the book might prevent the terrible face of suicide from coming into my life. We are so superstitious! I would not walk on cracks, would not take salt from another hand—it had to be put on the table first. I used thirteen as my lucky number, thinking to be lucky by refusing to be superstitious! Still, Clark was gone. The salt, the cracks, the numbers all had failed me.

Stephen Levine comforted and sustained me at many times during these last years. *Meetings at the Edge* and *Who Dies* were filled with powerful antidotes to my depression. It was with Levine that I first heard the phrase "most people leave skeletons in their closets when they die—the suicide leaves a skeleton in your closet." Professor Shneidman says it in a slightly different way. "The suicide leaves his psychological skeleton in your closet. You have to figure it out." Recently Susan Rose Baumer has written *How I Stayed Alive When My Brain Was Trying to Kill Me*, an excellent how-not-to book about her journey, in which she pulls together many of the habit changes that are necessary to a successful and full life in the face of suicidology, as Shneidman would call it.

I wrote in my journals every day, creating for myself a one-day-at-a-time survival manual, with prayers and promises, with memories and vows to live life as hard, as energetically, as I had tried to grieve. I began to remember, and to understand again, most of them, the lucky ones, are breaking their hearts and their backs and sometimes their necks to live. To live at any price.

JOURNAL ENTRY, JANUARY 19, 2000

Life is not for the faint of heart, and it is not for amateurs. It must be lived with spirit, which has nothing to do with physical health, in many cases. Being alive is full of terrible and wonderful things, and it takes commitment to live life on life's terms. It takes guts. And it takes a certain amount of the gambling instinct, I think, the sort of optimism that must be held out against evidence to the contrary. I have to make an attitude adjustment, I must "decide" that life is worth living, every day of my life, sometimes every moment.

And why not? What better point of view? That life is awful and unbearable? I think of life as beautiful, as wonderful and full of joy, and surprises, and vivid, psychedelic. Hieronymus Bosch pictured a world in which life is a mixed-up, vividly brutal, beautiful, mystifying universe, where men are, truly, barely civilized and under the skin, in the dark nights, awful beasts rout and burrow, desiring nothing more than to wreck our tiny bit of safety, burn our hastily built huts of grass, and make our lives miserable. I will be happy in spite of this, I have to say.

And the truth is, most of us have thought of suicide as an answer to some of our problems, at some time in our lives.

We might lack the nerve to commit the final act, and we might not recognize our "sinful" tendencies for what they are, but day in and day out we confront the problem of our innate attraction to self-destruction. We live in a world that encourages the small daily acts of negation that prepare us for the great one. . . . (Suicides) are not necessarily "sick" or "sinners," but simply our sisters and brothers. And who we are . . . the restless drifters, the walking wounded, may be nothing more than the steadfast commitment to sameness. The simplest form of suicide is the act of refusing the adventures and challenges that offer themselves to us every day.

— GEO STONE

Survivors of suicide are faced with the struggle to make a world again from one that has been shattered beyond recognition. That is true for survivors of all violent, sudden death, from murder, accidents, shocking sudden deaths without warning. But suicide is different. There are the centuries-old taboos that surround the issues of suicide. Suicide is different because people are mystified by the depths of the problems that suicide thrusts into their consciousness, and the facts of drug addiction, mental illness, alcoholism, insanity, and other subjects, difficult to face under more "normal" conditions, are thrust into the limelight and insist on being discussed. That is, if there is to be healing and peace and acceptance on the part of the survivor. At least this has been my experience.

Just as many people are allergic to mushrooms, and can be killed by shellfish, chocolate, berries, tomatoes, aspirin, and cheese, certain people are allergic to dust, molds, fungus, red foods (pepperine), dairy products, as well as pollens. Asthma, which can be fatal, is often caused by allergies to whatever is in the air around us, and may include allergies to microscopic bodies in the air, caused by everything from asbestos to mold. It stands to reason that people might also have vastly different reactions to drugs, antidepressants, and other substances that are used to fight depression.

Women in menopause often have deep depressions and difficult emotional balance. I found that I could not take any of the natural or chemically made forms of estrogen. Premarin put me on the floor with depression, and the use of the natural progesterone product made from South American yams, often found in creams and remedies for menopause, brought me down as well. Even testosterone, a hormone thought to enhance mood and offer other benefits for women who are in menopause, depressed me to the point of feeling suicidal. And I do not *feel* suicidal on a daily basis.

My mood swings are most always taken care of by daily rigorous exercise, both weight-bearing and impact aerobics like running, step-work and treadmill workouts. Since the age of twenty-six, when I understood that alcohol and many foods (not to mention life!) depressed me, I have been exercising on an average of five times a week. I wasn't to give up alcohol for another twelve years, but the exercise did wonders for my mood, even as I continued drinking. It may have been part of my denial structure, for if I had had to face the alcohol without exercise, I might have recognized its depressant qualities sooner, certainly before it started to tear my life apart. My bones are osteoporotic, but whatever is left is pretty strong, and I have been fortunate to not experience the deep emotional depressions described by many women in menopause.

Both exercise and meditation, doctors say, can stimulate an increase in the levels of serotonin in the body. Depression usually includes a decrease in the serotonin level, and I have read that people who are suicidal have lower levels of serotonin than most of us need for a balanced attitude. You can feel it. Before exercise, I may be down, not feeling like my optimistic self. After exercise, I am ready to take on the world. All has altered, and in what was formerly dark and unmanageable, I can now see light and possibility. It may not last for more than a day, but then the next day I can do the same thing, raise my serotonin levels. That is what medications do, as well. One day at a time.

They say there is a buildup over time in the natural approach, as well. In these years, my moods are dependable, because I do not introduce mood-depressants into my body (like alcohol and drugs), I meditate on a regular basis, and I exercise. This, over the years, has built confidence that I am in a stable and safe emotional place.

That, and a lot of other effort—writing, spending time in therapy, talking with friends, doing my work. As they said to me when I was in treatment, you stay sober, spend time with people who are also not drinking, and change your entire life!

Between the meditation, the exercise and doing work I love, my moods are usually steady and my attitude happy.

Depression is often said to be a result of the "brain disease" that Adina Wrobleski speaks of in her dissertations on the subject of suicide. Adina, who lives in Minnesota and knew friends of my son's, lost a daughter to suicide a few years before Clark's death. She has written many books about the brain disease that "causes" suicide, and feels that in most cases the treatment ought properly to be the new drugs made to change brain chemistry. Of course, drugs are not for everyone. The action of the heart can raise the level of serotonin, too, but meditation can achieve dramatic results for many people.

I have been struck by remarks of Dr. John Nash, the genius mathematician who suffered from depression and mental illness and about whom a movie and book have been made in recent years. *A Beautiful Mind* tells Dr. Nash's story. He had many violent and exploratory treatments at the hands of psychiatrists to alleviate his mental instability and deep depression. He had shock treatment and the brutal-sounding insulin treatments that were popular in some hospitals in the 1950s. He was put on many antipsychotic drugs and most people think he continues on drugs now, but that is not so. Dr. Nash decided he would use mind over matter, and for many years has been drug-free, having chosen to ignore the voices, the crowd that gathers in his mind and who told him to do what society calls crazy things. The deep depression disappeared and he looks and speaks as one who has overcome a great enemy and is leading a happy life at last. Of course, he could be the one exception to the rule that people cannot survive these mental disorders without drugs, but I do not believe that. I have suffered depression, certainly not to the degree that Dr. Nash has suffered, but for me, serious depression. I don't take drugs for depression. Of course, I drank for many years and was never aware that alcohol is a depressant.

I like Dr. Andrew Weil's prescription for depression, to "exercise heavily for thirty minutes (running, walking, jogging, swimming, jumping jacks) seven days a week and eat lots of broccoli." Basically, Andrew Weil and I agree. I think a diet free of alcohol, negativity, drugs, and depression can be the solution. Exercise, diet, and a connection to something greater than yourself—service in some area that helps others, for instance.

Of course, there are always mysteries. If having a strong religious connection is important, why is it that in Hungary, a Catholic country, the suicide rates are far higher on a regular basis than in the rest of Europe? Geo Stone notes that in both Hungary and Finland, which share the same rare linguistic heritage, Finno-Ugric, suicide rates are consistently high. Also, in Sri Lanka, during civil war, suicide rates jumped.

My son's gift to me, I would find, would be myself. Myself grieving, myself lifting the weights of life, the heavy burdens that come with getting up out of bed when you want to lie down and die with your lost loved one—the weights that make us search for music, for poetry, for our own creativity, to find our way; the weights that have to do with getting dressed instead of lying in bed wanting to die; of going to a shrink to talk about my losses rather than wallowing in my own pain; the heavy work that would make sure that I would not follow my son into my own grave, that I would sing, and write, that I would weep and cry and sob and shriek in the pain of losing him, and want to live for the two of us, instead of just me; the pain that would drive me to be with my family, to need my husband even more than ever, to hold my little fuzzy Persian cats in my arms and sob until their fur was soaked with my tears, that would move me to try, with all my heart, to continue my relationship with my granddaughter and my daughter-in-law, to try to make up in some way to my son's beloved daughter for the pain he had brought, and would bring, into her life. And into our families' lives.

I went out on the road, fighting to work, to survive, singing in all the places that I sing, traveling and trying to bring pleasure to myself and other people with my music. I felt the work was healing me. I knew the strength that was in the songs I sang, and the words I wrote. I knew that it was more important than ever to keep up my journals, writing when I wanted to scream, and screaming too, if that was what it would take. I cried with my mother, my sister, my brothers, my nephew, and my nieces. I wrote songs, sometimes, once I could bear to play the piano, weeping over the keys until they were slippery with tears. I sobbed into the white fur of my Persian cat, who was so patient and purred in consolation.

In my reading of recovery books, I found instructions for getting through a crisis or a loss—"Get a pet if you don't have one. Go to church." I went to church, St. John the Divine where Clark had knelt on the steps the morning he decided to go to treatment in Minnesota, where I had prayed for his sobriety. I sobbed in the pews while I listened to the music and the sound of the voices in the open spaces, amidst the marble and the stained glass, and the saints and music and smoke from the censers gave me comfort. I walked, everywhere I could, letting the cold air of winter wrap its arms around me in my black coat and high boots, and when it snowed I fell into the snow, making snow angels with my arms. I went to the mountains and walked among the wildflowers when the spring came. I walked around and around the lake at our house in the country, sometimes with Louis and often alone, in my running clothes. Sometimes I ran till I was out of breath, feeling the pounding of my heart beneath spandex, wanting to run until I couldn't breathe or think or feel anything other than my heart beating and my pulse flowing. I went swimming and swam with the pulse and rhythm of my arms and my legs putting oxygen into my bloodstream and taking away the sorrow.

I was lucky that there were also living miracles—friends, and my beautiful husband, Louis, whom I married a few years after Clark's death, for we had lived together for eighteen years and survived the worst and needed to express this in a ceremony of joy, and so we married. There was my loving family, my mom and brothers, Mike and David and Denver, and my sister, Holly, and their children, my nieces and nephews, whom I adore, and there is Hollis, Clark's daughter, to give me comfort and joy. She is blond and beautiful and full of light. And she is smart and cute and, when she was little, drew beautiful pictures and made everyone smile when she was around. She is pretty and kind and generous, like her father.

HOLLIS

I'm flying back from Providence, across the sea of green and gold, red and yellow—the leaves turning in autumn, the water's deep blue lakes curling through the October landscape like pointing fingers, floating scarves, meandering tangles of blue that reflect the sky and me in it. Flying—as usual.

I have been to see my granddaughter. I am giddy with pleasure, remembering the visit.

She runs down the red stone steps in her long blue dress, her blond hair long and flying behind her. She is wearing long blue wool stockings to her knees, which I don't see because of her skirt. Black tie shoes, one of which is trailing black laces. I refrain from telling her to tie her shoes. Let the others do that. I'm enthralled anyway and can't speak. "Nana, Nana!" she shouts so that all the world can hear. She hugs me and kisses me firmly on the lips. Her eyes are so full of blue, like the water. Like my eyes. Like her father's eyes, her mother's. Inside we find a hook for my bags, my ever-present wheely on the shelf underneath, the coat I have thankfully brought! The Moses Brown school is comforting and old, solid in its eighteenth-century buildings of brick and stone. I'm glad she is in a Quaker school. When I asked her about Moses Brown, when she had just started school at the end of the summer, who he was, she said—"A color?"

She whisks me into the classroom and introduces me to Seth and Virginia, her teachers. Fifteen children sit around the tables, and Holly pulls up a chair for me. Virginia passes out a quiz, and having not read the book, I answer all the questions anyway. It feels familiar. Very seldom, before the test, have I ever read the book in question anyway. Winging it, freewheeling, making it up as I go along is what it has always felt like. Making up my life as I go along. Now I realize most of us feel that way. No book of instructions before the test.

Side by side we sit, each writing. There is a big oak tree outside the window, gold and red and green. All the children have written autobiographies and Virginia tells me Holly shared her difficult story with the class.

"They'll find out anyway, why shouldn't they find out from me?" she tells her mother, Alyson. She loves deep books—the Brontes and Jack London, C. S. Lewis. The ones we read, all but the C. S. Lewis. Her skin is fairly breaking out of its pores, popping for all its worth. She's ten, going on nineteen. Trainer bra, steady now, but can the preteen roller coaster be far behind?

"She's always the same person, who you see is who you get," says Virginia. "But look out—at fourteen they all change!"

"Are you Jewish or are you Christian," a ten-year-old asks Seth during geography class. The children are coloring in maps of Rhode Island, concentrating on Washington County, where they live.

"I was raised Catholic," Seth says, "and that's not a question that's meant for public consumption." Catholics are unusual in this Quaker school, I guess.

I study the map, not having realized that Providence is on a deep inlet, far north of the coastline on a probing finger of water. I wonder how far I-95 is from the city. Holly's friend, Hanna, with whom she has just spent a few days in Florida, tells me, pointing generally south.

Hollis takes my hand when the firebell rings and we hurry outside for the drill, running into the chilly fall air with no coats, neither me nor the children. We hold hands on the way back, too, me and this lanky blond who is the vision, the shadow, the replica, of my son.

"I see the resemblance between you," says Virginia. She says it's mostly in the eyes. Hol and I look at each other, smiling, knowing. "And in certain other ways," I say for both of us. A two-hour love affair, when Mom comes to take me out to lunch. I am sitting at the table with Holly and Hanna and Laura and Nino, showing them my answers to the quiz. We are giggling. When Mom appears—a frown on my face. Such a sad parting.

I can't wait till I see her next, when I shall once again wear a grandmother's heart on my sleeve.

·   ·   ·

A friend asked me recently if it gives me pain when the women around me talk about their children—this one going to college, that one getting married, this son off to his first big job in England, that one having a baby. I say no, it doesn't upset me. I want to scream and shout and cry and throw things, but I don't. I have done that already, made my peace with Clark's choice.

Or so I think, from time to time. Until the arrow lodges in my heart again. Until the next dream in which he comes to me so powerfully, as though he were in the room with me. Until I see a mother with a little boy, redheaded, walking in a park or a mall or an airport, see her bend down to wipe his nose or straighten his little jacket. Then my heart breaks, again and again. How many times can your heart break? Forever, your heart can break forever. Letting in the sorrow, and letting out the rage. Break, my heart, till all the tears are gone. Break, my heart, till all the hope is restored. Break, till all the days that he is not here are over; break until he returns.

I have learned that no suicide attempt is ever a rehearsal, but a scream for help, and that anyone with suicidal tendencies should get professional help.

They say that if you are an alcoholic, you are probably ten times as likely to kill yourself as those who are not addicted to alcohol or drugs, and so you must learn about suicide and what the act does to your loved ones. Perhaps if there is any prevention possible, it will come with the understanding of the chaos, the pain, the tears, the horror, and the hurt that is inflicted on survivors by their loved ones who have taken their own lives.

Healing comes, and time passes. Nothing can ever make up for Clark's death, but his beautiful blond daughter, Hollis, who looks exactly like him but is her own amazing and unique person, will always lift my heart.

In Geo Stone's book, *Suicide and Attempted Suicide*, he says that in most cases, those who intend to kill themselves do just that, and therapy, as well as other means of support, seldom prevents a determined individual from taking his own life if he determines to do so. "Though often useful, professional help is no guarantee against suicide."

But taking time to live your life and celebrate and do the things that are healing can just possibly save yours.

CHAPTER 15

Choosing *to* Live Beyond Despair

For years I've practiced ritual,
It's dead now.
For years, I've practiced meditation,
It's dull now.
Finally, there is only soaring
Like a ribbon
Floating over the sea.
Like a dragon, soaring in the air.

—MING-DAO DENG,

TAO: DAILY MEDITATIONS

I came to understand, in my early twenties, that the hole in my heart could bring on depression. In William Styron's important book, *Darkness Visible: A Memoir of Madness,* he ends with what is almost a hymn to the good news of depression and its impact on those of us who suffer from the condition.

Men and women who have recovered from the disease—and they are countless—bear witness to what is probably its only saving grace: it [depression] is conquerable.

For those who have dwelt in depression's dark wood, and known its inexplicable agony, their return from the abyss is not unlike the ascent of the poet, trudging upward and upward out of hell's black depths and at last emerging into what he saw as "the shining world." There, whoever has been restored to health has almost always been restored to the capacity for serenity and joy, and this may be indemnity enough for having endured the despair beyond despair.

I was traveling with my concerts, going out into the world again, and singing. I had a feeling that every concert was a sort of healing session for my heart, as well as for others. On the road, I wrote in my journals, spending time on the computer while the planes flew and the cars drove. The writing soothed me, and the questions I had, when I wrote them down, seemed to find answers of their own. I thought long and deep about my own suicide attempt, and about depression, and wrote about these thoughts. I would have to talk about these things with the group, I thought.

Depression, I wrote, is the original and constant battlefield, and, for me, the prelude to suicidal thoughts. Now, from the reading and the work I have done on suicide and the why of suicide, I realize that what I have called depression in my later years is not the same thing that drove me to my first attempt. I had what Shneidman calls psychache. And I found a therapist and spent many years really talking about what ailed me, and he, and she, found out what hurt and found out how to help me. In a way, it was that simple. And that complicated.

I use every tool I have, and they work—meditation, diet, exercise, friends, therapy, work. Whether I am depressed or not means the difference between living in peace and harmony, or living in a place that resembles the lost regions of another world. Its presence can determine whether I am filled with joy and serenity, or on the edge of madness. The road, as they say, gets narrower the longer I stay alive.

A poem by Charlie Smith, "Family Plot," shakes my winter armor, rattles the icy cover—

He was the saddest case . . . a boy starving at the feast . . .
keeping his uncomplicated vigil before the cannons of the dark.

Oh God, let me not starve at the feast. Let me believe in the awakening, the coming of the winter sun after the solstice. No matter how dark this winter has been, let me feel the nourishment of the feast in the light of the new dawn, the return of the sun, the new beginning.

Most doctors say artistic people suffer a greater proportion of depression and suicidal thinking, that sensitive, deep-thinking artists suffer more. I think we are all artistic in our own ways, and that many of us, artists and non-artists alike, have places where reality shears off into addiction, mental conflict, mental illness, fear and pain. Life is, after all, hard. And there exists a very fine line, a thin, permeable membrane between the forces of destruction and the forces of creation.

A lot of us who suffer depression also celebrate life with

our creativity. My friends and I, artists, singers, painters alike, have talked about this narrow road, pitted with stones, where joy and creativity are often plagued with the demons of the dark side, as well as flung to the heavenly light of making something beautiful, meaningful, important in the world.

In *The World of C. G. Jung*, its authors, Stephen Segaller and Merrill Berger, say of the work of this master psychologist and one of the seminal forces in the ideas behind the book and the movement, *Alcoholics Anonymous*:

> . . . he noticed that for many in the second half of life, the essential psychological problem could be described as religious; and . . . personal religion, and a sense of meaning, was an undeniable aspect of the human psyche. . . .He wanted to revalue the very idea of psychological instability, or pain, as a potentially creative process—for us to recognize that depression, dreams and conflict all tell us something important which we need to hear.

I have read of the causes of suicide—of mental disorders, chemical imbalances. I have read about shock therapies used in previous times, of horrible penalties imposed on the families of suicides and on suicides themselves. I have read of the condemnation of suicides by churches and synagogues.

I still find it hard to believe that a society could take revenge on someone who is sick, and on his or her family, yet only the other day I was talking to a Jewish friend who told me that it was close to impossible to find a synagogue in Manhattan that would perform a ceremony for the funeral of a Jew who had committed suicide.

True, it was St. Augustine who said, "No man may inflict death upon himself at will, merely to escape from temporal difficulties." During the years of St. Augustine's writing *The City of God*, suicide was thought to be caused by the devil. So it is not surprising that religion does not have more of a healing effect on the soul-searching that is required by someone who is suicidal. No more than any of us, I suppose, but with more urgency, perhaps.

In all the reading I have done, I have come across only minimal reference to the idea that it is possible that suicide ideology may be the result of an old-fashioned crisis of faith in the person suffering from the conviction that taking their own life is an appropriate solution. Nearly no one talks these days of this issue of faith anyway, and there are few references to the soul, except among the writings of Jung and James Hillman and a handful of others.

Jung says, "To me it seemed that one's duty was to explore daily the will of God."

I don't read much in suicide writing about going to a spiritual advisor, or a church group, or a group for healing with the idea of asking a "power greater than ourselves" to take this compulsion away, this compulsion to self-destruct. A power greater than ourselves can be anything, from the group itself to the doorknob to the return to religious practices from childhood to following a new and refreshing alternative to the early God-fearing, Bible-thumping days of a punishing God. Most of my reading today asks us to make up a kinder, more loving impression of who God is to us. There are groups to help you not to smoke a day at a time, not to drink, use drugs, gamble, eat, act out sexually, not spend money compulsively. Groups to help you survive suicide and not take your life, one day at a time.

Two years ago, I went to Washington for a workshop on mental health, run by then Vice President Al Gore and his wife, Tipper Gore. It was profoundly moving, with many people talking about their personal experiences in mental illness of all kinds, including depression. Mike Wallace spoke openly, as did Tipper herself, of having had to find solutions for their illness of depression. Since then, I have wondered if there shouldn't be a day of national awareness of suicide prevention in the United States. It would mean a society that intends to talk about mental health, depression, drug addiction, alcohol abuse, spouse and child abuse at a national and personal level, and a society that wants to break out of denial. Except in rare instances, despite many programs and brave people like the Gores and Mike Wallace, William Styron, Patty Bosworth, Mariette Hartley, and others who have written and spoken out about suicide, I don't think we are there yet.

What is the secret to daily living? Simple. It is daily dying.

—JOE AND CHARLIE, SPEAKERS ON

THE 12 STEPS OF ALCOHOLICS ANONYMOUS

JOURNAL ENTRY, DECEMBER 1992, COLORADO

December, cold, freezing after rain, sheets of ice on the trees, sheaths like silver armor, crystals shaking in the wind. The sun in its short zenith passes into night so quickly, no time to melt the snow in its visit. The cold hunkers down like a vagabond in a big coat, waiting out the night, till morning. And morning is so far away.

But tomorrow, as the sun breaks through the ice, Christmas morning will be nearer. Our promise blinks like the crystals of light from the trees, from the house, from the mountaintops, the promise of the returning sun, the coming Christ, the promise that life is renewed, reborn. The gifts lie under the tree, waiting, purple and gold, silver and red, we greet the new dawn with music and with celebration. Memorializing you, in this celebration and festivity that has everything in it. Except you. And everything reminds me, you are not here to share in the winter, where candles light our joy together. My poor son, who saw only the ice, only the darkness, only the end of light.

For today, one day at a time, I do not think of suicide, I don't go there. I am sober, I take the steps every day that will keep me sane and connected to people.

But I know my suicidal feelings are not ever conquered entirely. There are drugs for depression, of course, and one can take them. I don't. But the work has to go on, with or without them.

The work. What is the work? What is the work for someone who knows suicide, has survived his own attempt or someone else's? I think the most important thing for me is to know there are other choices, that getting permanently out of my pain is not the only answer. There are friends, therapists, habits of work and of life that take the power out of the depression.

For me, prayer removes the black dog; writing, singing,

working, seeing friends takes away depression; doing my work, playing the piano, going to the gym, just moving, walking in the park seems to lift the depression. I know when I do these things I increase the levels of serotonin in my body, and I know that people who are depressed and who are suicidal have levels of serotonin that are too low. These can be raised with drugs, but they can also be raised with activity in the body.

I struggled with the black apparition from my childhood, apparently for no reason. I could feel it hover, feel its claws tighten on my throat, my heart, defying every rational thought, making a mockery of optimism, of good fortune, of anything true and valuable and real. It is as though, from time to time, the black dog had to come to be fed its share, to be petted, paid attention to, bribed to slink off or shown the back of my hand, the steel of my resolve, the smile of my angels.

If I don't exercise for a couple of days, I feel the shadow's edge, and as the days go on, the whole shadow, and the deep depression, will emerge. If I eat too much sugar, it rears its head as I wake, desperate to get me thinking of the negative. If I don't go to a group of people who are recovering from alcoholism and talk about the "ism" of the disease, the reasons we drank— the seven deadly sins of greed, anger, envy, lust, gluttony, sloth, and pride—I feel it creep around my heart and threaten to pull me down in my tracks. I feel it when I am ill with a flu, fondling my heart, pulling down my soul, stalking my joy with its dark face.

In the years when I drank, I was in many hotel rooms, in many cities, in many countries. Some harbored the howl of the black dog. There were decades of nights I thought I wouldn't make it back out of the dog's dark cave, many years when the sunlight didn't make any difference. I learned the black dog has no address, but can follow me anywhere. I just have to have face him with my own light and with all the weapons I know. I have many weapons against despair and against suicide today. One of these is an attempt to stay close to God. Drugs had played a part in my own twenty-three-year drinking story, and I took acid and sleeping pills and uppers and downers, all the booze I could drink and all the denial I could swallow, and anything I could get my hands on to change my mood.

None of us knows how much pain we really can bear. What if I had cancer or some other dread disease? What about euthanasia? If I cannot bear to live in some particular way, what does it matter if the pain is emotional or physical? It is a right. I think alcohol may have saved my sanity. Isn't that strange, for I tried to kill myself before I started drinking. But I had intense, day-in, day-out therapy, in which I settled for the long suicide of drinking, to get away from the black dog, not knowing the alcohol had the dog on a leash as long as I was drinking.

But the black dog lived on every shore. When I was drinking, I tried many things, including one-night stands, which did not help, as I always hoped they would. Often, instead of helping a depression, they made it worse.

Although I have been told that depression can be treated with drugs, I have never had any experience with antidepressants. I will only tell you what I know of my own journey to the edge of that precipice.

So, though I don't take drugs for my depression, I know the physical benefit of endorphins, when they are running around my body, during and after a swiftly moving workout on the treadmill or running around the lake or sweating in my hotel room, running from room to room.

Most of the time, after I spend a half-hour or more exercising, depression lifts the dark cloud so completely that I feel a small miracle has been accomplished. Only it is no small miracle, it is very real, and a matter of life and death. In the treatment of depression, Dr. Andrew Weil advises, as do other physicians, "avoidance of alcohol, sedatives, antihistamines, and other depressant drugs." After many years of not using drugs and alcohol, I can see their direct connection to the depression I experienced when I was abusing both, never happy in any emotional state, always looking for a way out. Dr. Weil also talks about dietary modification—less protein and fat, more fruits and vegetables. There are foods I know I am allergic to, that make me depressed and I have to avoid them. Sugar, sometimes grain and wheat.

Mental illness can be confusing in an active or recovering alcoholic or drug addict, because when I was using, I was acting in an insane manner much of the time. When I was detoxed from the booze and the drugs, I started acting like the rest of the planets, sometimes up, sometimes down, but not as depressed. There is research now that tells us those tendencies to depression and chemical dependency are often inherited. And if these are chemical imbalances, we can address them. I now know that I can use my own chemistry to change my feelings, lift my dark shadows. And so, a knowledge of the effects of what I eat and the role of alcohol and drugs in depression is a *must* if I want to be conscious, if I am to take my mental and physical health into my own hands. This is a relatively new concept, and most of us have depended on the medical community for so long to pull us in and out of emotional as well as physical symptoms with drugs, that we feel strange being proactive in our search for health.

With meditation and exercise and prayer, I began to learn slowly how to send the black dog howling into the woods, slinking home.

The tools against the black dog of depression—running, swimming, meditation, writing in journals, talking, eating right, sleeping, creating—have helped me to recover from my son's death.

I have been fortunate that on the road to health I have discovered those who journeyed before me, pioneers I could trust and emulate. If someone has recovered from a symptom or a condition that I have suffered, I am eager to know how, especially if they have found a natural, noninvasive means to health.

I have found recovery, joy, tremendous gratitude, and the knowledge that the stars are always shining somewhere. I have only to look through the blue sky or into the black night to find them and let them shine on me. The sky will clear, my mind will clear, if I move from negative to positive. In the moment of silence between stars, there is healing, there is the sound of the pulse of light, the sound of God talking to me, listening to me, healing me, bringing me strength. All I have to do is look up.

Finding our way through the darkness and pain of depression is the path to our brilliant days. Running with the black dog may lead us to a place of wonder and light and joy that we may not otherwise have seen.

Run black dog, along my side,
Along the river where the raindrops slide
Along the cliff,
Along the hill,
Along the path
Where the air is still
Run till we're both
Out of breath and time
And life has poured
One more sweet wine
Onto the skin
Onto the heart,
Onto the sky where the
Raindrops start
Run with me to the end of our run
To the place where time and pain are one
Tell me no stories
Tell me no lies
I can live where the black dog flies.

CHAPTER 16

Healing Waters—
Sanity *and* Grace

As for suicide, it is a terrible but utterly natural reaction to the strained, narrow, unnatural necessities we sometimes create for ourselves.

—A. ALVAREZ

A thousand people are officially dead of suicide every day, but they are not the only ones who are faced with the constant choice between life and death. We all are.

—EDWIN SHNEIDMAN

Although life will never be the same, there are gifts that have come in the years since Clark died. I am often blissful, and peaceful, or at times heartbroken. All can exist, so I have found, in the same moment, in the same heartbeat.

Suicide, it seems, touches everyone in some way. Whenever

the subject comes up, there is always talk of this or that loved one, a relative whose suicide was hidden, the long tentacles of pain and shame that attend to those who, not even knowing the details, are the inheritors of family sorrow and loss that in many cases have no name.

I recently heard one of the reasons that people are eager to speed us over the course of our grief. It was Emily Post, who finally put the dodge on grief—Stop it! Get on with your life! You don't want to bring everyone down, do you? Don't they say to you, When are you going to get on with your life? When is this preoccupation, and this mourning, going to be over?

Ten years have passed since my son's suicide. I am living a life of acceptance and of gratitude that I had Clark with me for the thirty-three years he was in my life. But I think I am more, rather than less, interested in the subject of the last taboo of suicide than I was in my early grief. The first grief has passed, in some ways. I loved and treasured my son. I love my life, I revel in my work and in my friendships and my most precious marriage to an understanding and intelligent man whom I adore and who helped me through my grief. I have, through the luck and whim of the Universe, and whatever Gods are operating in my favor, a wonderful life and a successful marriage.

Every one of us has the "right" to end our lives on our own timetable. Don't we? And most of us are helpless to prevent, predict, intervene, or influence the life and death of a would-be suicide.

Suicide is the last taboo. Suicide is the inalienable right of all human beings, they say. Really? According to the philosopher, Richard W. Momeyer,

Suicide is an act that does not occur in a vacuum . . . Having
a right to do something provides us some entitlement to do it; it
does not assure that doing it is right. It is appropriate to set
very high standards of justification for exercising a right to
suicide, given how often it is undertaken in an ill-considered
manner, how frequently suicides suffer diminished competence
from mental illness, and how widespread and serious (and often
devastating) are the consequences for others.

Professor Shneidman has written many of the important
books about suicide that have become available in the last fifty
years. According to Shneidman, as well as other sources, in
those cases that are recorded in the medical annals of emergency
rooms and doctors' offices, there are strong links between mental illness and suicide, between alcoholism and suicide, and between depression and suicide.

"Suicide haunts our literature and our culture," Shneidman
says in his 1996 book, *The Suicidal Mind:*

[Suicide] is the taboo subtext to our successes and our happi-
ness. The reporting of a suicide of any public figure disturbs
each of us. Amid our dreams of happiness and achievement lurk
our nightmares of self-destruction. Who is not mindful of the
potential self-defeating elements with our own personality? The
world is full of dangers, but it is the threat of self-destruction
that we are most afraid to touch, except in our secret moments
or the hidden recesses of our minds. Yet suicide happens every
day, and many people we know have had a relative or friend
who has committed suicide.

Suicide is a spiritual as well as a physical subject.

Suicide can be a final act at the end of a long illness; it can be a mistake, an overdose of drugs or alcohol that might likely kill on their own merits; it can be harbored in the soul, a seed that thrives on depression and negativity, or is fed by the family myths, both real and imagined, of other suicides within the family. Suicide is sometimes an act of political terrorism, sometimes an act of war. Suicide always leaves us bewildered. It always leaves us with questions, and with the desire, in some of us, to take our own lives as a solution to our pain.

Since the events of 9/11, there has been a steady increase in suicides among all ages and genders. Suicide can turn us homicidal. It can destroy families, destroy myths; it can also create myths.

"An act like this," said Camus, "is prepared within the silence of the heart, as is a great work of art." I believe the silence is one of the great problems. Suicide is usually only whispered about, never quite shouted, as it should be, to the rooftops

Artists and non-artists alike take their own lives. Children, people who are ill, who are lost, who are sick, who otherwise appear well and healthy, take their own lives. Those of us who are touched by the terror of suicide know that the veil of secrecy can kill the suicide, as well as those who love him or her. And we know that much of the material of suicide is also that of life. As Michael Bakunin, the Russian political theorist and anarchist, said, "The passion for destruction is also a creative passion." So many artists, so many young, talented, beautiful men and women have taken their own lives. So many pained men and women of every age, so many uncertain, struggling, lost, and sometimes found human beings for whom the act of living is too painful to pursue. Or for whom the act of suicide is a brilliant solution to an otherwise insoluble mystery.

We all need assurance that we can speak of the journey, and therefore heal the dreadful loss, or the private knowledge that suicide can be a choice, or a result of illness, but it is not always a foregone conclusion.

Suicide has the power to destroy, but also to create new conditions of reality. And no one of us needs be alone.

As Professor Shneidman says—

"Suicide prevention can be . . . everybody's business."

The Eternal Light

At first, I saw only a deep chasm, where there was nothing but blackness before me, in back of me, in front of me. Memories were enemies, pushing me to the edge, forcing me to lose my balance, black out, slip from the center of time into a black place of pain. Somewhere in that blackness there was a light, a presence, that was your bright spirit, on this side, and on that side, and on every side of the tragedy of your loss. I love your spirit, as I loved your self, with all my heart, with all my soul; as I could see you more and more in the dark, I felt the memories come to me not as forces of darkness but as forces of healing and light.

Surrender, letting go, accepting, reaching in, forgiving, hurting when it hurts and smiling when I am happy, crying when the tears come, and laughing, for the bliss of being with you on this side and that; for love, from the beginning till now, and till forever. God gave you to me. God has taken you from me, but has left me your spirit. Tonight, as the moon rose into the black velvet sky studded with stars, the memories of you were brighter than the stars, and your spirit more beautiful. In my dark sky, filled with the memories of stars, you are brightest tonight.

Just as nothing in the universe is ever lost, Clark is as near as my imagination. He will always be my child. I talk to him, we discuss the reasons for his death, I ask his advice, and I thank him for helping me to get through the days. Sometimes we are angry with each other, sometimes he says I have failed him, sometimes I accuse him of failing me, of trying to destroy me. But we are talking, learning from each other as we did in life. He says, This is my journey, not yours, and I tell him it is hard to see a difference. We fight, we make up, we laugh, and we love, in death as in life. Sometimes there is no partition at all, as in some nights when my dreams are as real as his breath, his pulse, and his smile.

There are no guarantees in this journey, and we do not know how the communication is supposed to come, what is appropriate or what is not. Who says that what my son has to teach me cannot be done from another sphere? I don't know that.

All I have to do is think of you; there you are, in my dreams, in my thoughts, in my life, in my body, in my universe. You are here, you are there, and we are, as we have always been, together.

I have always believed in spirits, in the life beyond what we can see and touch. The light of candles burned in my nights when I sat in prayer, when the spirit of my son would come into the light, like an angel of old, and shine on me as though his body and his spirit were burning, as though my son's whole life were on fire in front of me, not with fire from earth, but with heavenly fire that seemed to burn the pain out of me, seemed to burn the longing out of me, and the fear. I could get through these nights, I could even sleep, because he was close to me, near me, as near as my breath, as near as the candle flame that stood between me and the darkness. He stood between me and the darkness. He and the candlelight stood between me and my own death. I traveled the country, singing my concerts, hearing the sound of my own heart beating in the tone of my voice, and when I did, I was lifted, as though on the flame of that candle I burned each night, lifted and held safe from those ghosts in the corners. And the songs I sang were a scream that came out music, melody, and moved into the air with the smoke from the candles. Singing held me, like the light, like my son's spirit hovering over me at night as I slept—held me from death.

The reflection of light from the candle's flame would move in my hair and in the still room, lighting up the corners where the ghosts hid themselves when it was daylight. At night they came out of hiding, and only the firelight and the burning spirit of my son in front of the candles held them back. In those first nights after his death he would come to me and he would tell me things, secrets, his voice startling me out of my meditations, as clear and as clarion as a bell. His familiar and beloved voice came, telling me to beware, to take care of myself, to be kind to myself, that he loved me, that I was not to blame.

I have always believed in ghosts. I believe Clark's ghost came to me after he took his own life. He was settling things here, with me, with others. His ghost, or his spirit. My mother, when her father died, told me he came to the foot of her bed, where she was living in Los Angeles. He died in Seattle, but that night he came to her and he appeared, as ghosts are said to do. He stood there, letting her see that he was fine, that he was all right. Just so did my son appear to me in those first nights, telling me that he was all right. Telling me that I was all right.

A friend, when my son died, sent me a note that said, "God has reserved a special place of love and tenderness for people who have suffered so much in their lives. There, they are in everlasting love, everlasting bliss, everlasting joy."

Today Clark's beautiful family is surviving, and thriving. I live with the memory and the spirit of my son and his death each day, and each day I wake up surprised, once again, that this is now the path I walk. I do not dwell in dark, shadowed corners. I have learned from him that my secrets can kill me. I want to live life to the fullest, the only revenge there is. I want to celebrate, to make joy and service the purpose of my life. I will transcend tragedy. This is my promise to my son, so that I can live out his dreams, in a way, and my own, for a fresh start, a new day.

The healing comes in waves, and some days are still dark and frightening. But I know I am healing.

I felt the change powerfully one night, a few months after Clark's death, when my beloved friend and husband Louis and I and some friends were having dinner in a happy, crowded restaurant. I was still thin and shaky, and wasn't sleeping well. Suddenly, in the room of friends and strangers, amid bright-colored glass and candlelight, gleaming faces of people I knew and loved, I heard a laugh, a resonant bell, deep and full of pleasure. It was coming from a voice that sounded familiar. It took me more than a little while to realize it was my voice, laughing.

It was me, stepping into life again.

Epilogue

On a brilliant day in June of 2003, we dedicated Clark's bench on the grounds of Hazelden in Center City, Minnesota. In the sun and shadow, Clark's daughter and many of his friends and family members were gathered. Each spoke of our memories of my bright, beautiful, soulful son, and as the words of the Serenity Prayer filled the bright air, I heard a red-winged blackbird sing in the nearby trees and watched swallows fly in and out of the tangle of green trees and plants by the lake. Clark loved this place and the songs of the birds. He fished the rivers up there in Minnesota and learned many lessons. His bench, designed by Louis Nelson with some input by me, is a long lounge of polished granite, with a round stone pillow engraved with Clark's name and dates. "Beloved son, husband, father, nephew, cousin, friend," it reads. The bench is sited under a single pine tree by the lake, near the entrance path to the walk through the woods that is used by many recovering alcoholics and addicts as they pause to reflect, to run or walk, listening to the birds and feeling the beauty of this place of peace and recovery. The light sparkled on the water, and one lone heron stood on a leg in the shallow water, listening, it seemed, to the story of my son's life. We talked of Clark's humor and kindness, his love of sobriety, his struggle to live and love and be of service. He helped so many people in his life, and in his death the help he gave lives on in me, in his friends, in his family, and in the life of his daughter. To have my granddaughter there, listening to the voices of those who loved her father the most, and hearing their stories of this wonderful, loving man, was one of the greatest gifts of my life.

Our hard-won lessons—to live life to the very fullest and be filled with joy—shivered in the leaves of the bright green trees and the eyes shining around me. Someone will sit on the bench, I am sure, and play a guitar. Tears will fall there, and laughter echo.

My son's spirit lives on.

A Bibliographical Guide

As I worked on *Sanity and Grace* over the years after my son's death, I tried to read everything I could find on suicide. I sought out new writers, looked for articles and personal stories, and often would go to a bookstore or a library and just browse—looking for any book that talked about how to live through the trauma and taboo. In the aftermath of my son's death, I asked members of our family and close friends to get together and talk about their own personal experiences of suicide. Much healing was found among us then, as well as in the months and years that followed.

Included in the bibliography are books that I have found essential to healing and learning to live fully after the tragedy of suicide. The list is in alphabetical order, rather than chronological, because I found it hard to order each one's importance in my life. Yet all of these books have been healing and helpful to me at different times and for different reasons.

Alcoholics Anonymous, or The Big Book as it is referred to by members of the program, leads off the list, because it is "A" and because I have found it to be the finest road to a change in attitudes one could hope for, whether dealing with drugs, alcohol, food, relationships, fear, depression, or any other problem I might have. When reading, I change the word "alcohol" to anything I wish to have lifted, and I work the twelve steps of AA on whatever the problem is. They say that in life it is not what happens to us but how we react to life's situations that matters. The Big Book has helped change my attitudes toward what life brings me.

For me, the "spiritual" aspect of recovery cannot be emphasized too much, and therefore I have included books that might serve as a guide to the inner journey I have needed to take.

The Bible should be added to this list, particularly the Book of Psalms, which, by reading, I can walk through darkness to light, move from pain to joy.

I cannot live without Emmet Fox, and the I Ching. And the writings of Stephen Levine have been like handrails over the raging river, taking me safely through dark days and nights. The men and women who have shared their journeys of suicide in their books have given us a road map of courage—Iris Bolton and Mariette Hartley, Gloria Vanderbilt and Sue Chance, William Styron and Joan Rivers, Patricia Bosworth and Calvin Trillin, and many others have helped lift us over roaring waters and chasms of sorrow.

As the years have gone by, I have found new books that shed more light and helped me see that my loss is not personal, yet it is the most personal thing I may ever survive, thus thriving instead of just surviving. Some books I have known for years; others, like *No Time to Say Goodbye*, I have just found. Every day I need to be reading something that will explain, or comfort me spiritually, or just let me rage at the loss, or cheer at the possibilities of life. We all have losses, and daily we die, in meditation we die, and therefore find the strength to live.

I have been led, as though by healing angels, to books and people who have helped. My friend George Furth sends me every article he can find on suicide and its impact on young and old alike. It was he who sent me an in-depth piece by Tom Curwin in the *Los Angeles Times* about Dr. Edwin Shneidman and gave me the courage to call Dr. Shneidman and begin what I now count as an important friendship with this kind and brilliant healer and suicidologist.

There are groups that can help as well. I have not listed them because they change too often to be reliable, although Compassionate Friends is an organization that can help, and Survivors of Suicide (SOS) has branches all over the country. If you go online and do a search on Google, you can find groups in your city and resources that can be helpful. Iris Bolton's Link counseling group in Atlanta supports healing by putting families together, and letting them find their own dynamic in recovery.

An enlightened minister or counselor from your church, synagogue, mosque, or spiritual center can help, if you trust his or her humanity. With your honesty, you might even help him or her. People need to talk about suicide, and we are the ones who can lead the way.

You can start your own family healing by gathering family members and speaking of your loved one and of your feelings about losing this person to suicide. And if you yourself feel suicidal, as many of us do after a traumatic loss or even simply from time to time because these feelings are natural, not only for a depressed or ill person but for all of us, there are hotlines in cities all over the country. If you dial 911, you will be referred to people who can help you live through this one day at a time. Help is out there. You can reach for it.

You can create for yourself a strong, flexible, and caring network, with friends and supportive groups and individuals, as well as books that bring you comfort, so that you will not be alone in your loss. You have inner strengths; the "eye inside you that sees all" knows what you must do, and you can do it.

You have probably noticed that if you bring up the subject of suicide in a gathering of any number of people, nearly all of them will have some personal experience of suicide within their family or among their friends. Often people will remember a suicide that has been long forgotten and as they speak of it, there may be a sudden chill in the room, as though everyone's heart had stopped beating for a moment. People are seldom able to share much about the loss or their feelings around their particular suicide. Guilt, shame, fear, and the inability to understand why the person did it will often be a part of their sharing. They seem to be crippled in some emotional way by the unprocessed experience. Keeping suicide a secret appears to me to be a bit like not having a tumor taken out and looked at by a doctor, or not taking a blood test when you know you have been exposed to some dangerous disease. If we don't take actions, the pain and guilt and shame fester and can often make us emotionally ill.

I believe the attitude about suicide today is much the same as the attitude about cancer was three decades ago. People did not want to talk about cancer, and knew very little about how it could be prevented, detected, treated, and often cured. Those of us who have experienced suicide are faced with a social taboo. Each of us has a responsibility to say "Here and no further with the taboo business—we will talk about this and deal with it and go as deep as we must, but the taboo ends with me!"

If any of these books help you, all the better. The most important thing I know is that they helped me face the truth, and truth is where the end of the taboo and the start of healing begins.

Judy Collins's Suggested Reading List

Alcoholics Anonymous
Alcoholics Anonymous World
Services, Inc.
1996

Around the Year with Emmet Fox
Emmet Fox
Harper & Row
1958

Breaking the Silence
Mariette Hartley, Anne Commire
Putnam Publishing Group
1990

Children of Jonah
Edited by James T. Clemons
Capital Books, Inc.
2001
Foreword by Judy Collins

Darkness Visible: A Memoir of Madness
William Styron
Random House
1990

Good Grief: Healing Through
the Shadow of Loss
Deborah Morris Coryell
The Shiva Foundation
1997

How I Stayed Alive When My Brain Was
Trying to Kill Me: One Person's
Guide to Suicide Prevention
Susan Rose Blauner
Morrow
2002

In the Midst of Winter
Edited by Mary Jane Moffat
Vintage Books
1992

Lao Tzu / Tao Te Ching
Translated by John C. H. Wu,
  Edited by Paul K. T. Sih
St. John's University Press
1961

Letters of the Scattered Brotherhood
Edited by Mary Strong
Harper & Row
1948

Meeting at the Edge
Stephen Levine
Anchor Books
1984

My Son . . . My Son . . . A Guide to
  Healing After Death, Loss, or Suicide
Iris Bolton with Curtis Mitchell
Bolton Press
1983

No Time to Say Goodbye: Surviving the
  Suicide of a Loved One
Carla Fine
Main Street Books, Doubleday
1999

The Noonday Demon: An Atlas
  of Depression
Andrew Solomon
Scribner
2001

On Suicide: Great Writers on the
  Ultimate Question
Edited by John Miller
Chronicle Books
1992

The Savage God: A Study of Suicide
A. Alvarez
Norton
1990

Shattered
Jeanette Mason
Copyright Jeanette Mason
1999
Available at
  www.jeanettemason.com

Silent Grief: Living in the Wake of Suicide
Christopher Lukas and Henry M.
  Seiden, Ph.D.
Scribner
1987

The Spirituality of Imperfection:
  Storytelling and the Journey
  to Wholeness
Ernest Kurtz and Katherine
  Ketcham
Bantam Books
1994

Stronger than Death
Sue Chance, M.D.
Norton
1992

Suicide and Attempted Suicide
Geo Stone
Carroll & Graf Publishers
1999

Suicide and the Soul
James Hillman
Sixth Spring Publications
1990

The Suicidal Mind
Edwin S. Shneidman
Oxford University Press
1996

*Suicide: Why? 85 Questions and
    Answers about Suicide*
Adina Wrobleski
Afterwords
1989

Suicide and Life-Threatening Behavior
    (Journal)
Surviving Suicide (Quarterly
    Newsletter)
American Association of
    Suicidology
www.suicidology.org

*Unfinished Business: Pressure Points
    in the Lives of Women*
Maggie Scarf
Ballantine Books
1980

Vagabond House
Don Blanding
Applewood Books
2002

What Does the Bible Say About Suicide?
James T. Clemons
Fortress Press
1990

When Bad Things Happen to Good People
Harold S. Kushner
Schocken Books
1989

*Who Dies? An Investigation of Conscious
    Living and Conscious Dying*
Stephen Levine
Doubleday
1982

Why Suicide
Eric Marcus
HarperSanFrancisco
1996

ABOUT THE AUTHOR

JUDY COLLINS is celebrating her forty-fourth year of recording, with forty albums, several top-ten hits, Grammy nominations, and gold and platinum status. She received an Academy Award nomination for her film, *Antonia: A Portrait of the Woman*, and recently started her own label, Wildflower Records, which contributes a portion of its proceeds to charity and nonprofit organizations. The author of *Trust Your Heart, Singing Lessons, Voices, Amazing Grace, The Judy Collins Songbook,* and the novel *Shameless,* she lives in New York.